Paul's Mission to Asia Minor and Greece

FROM PERSECUTOR TO *Apostle*

FROM PERSECUTOR TO *Apostle*

A BIOGRAPHY OF PAUL

THOMAS A. WAYMENT

SALT LAKE CITY, UTAH

To Brandi,
for filling my life with joy and happiness
(October 2, 1984)

All photos were taken by the author.

Visit us at deseretbook.com

Library of Congress Cataloging-in-Publication Data

Wayment, Thomas A.
From persecutor to Apostle : a biography of Paul / Thomas A. Wayment.
p. cm.
Includes bibliographical references and index.
ISBN-10 1-59038-617-5 (hardbound : alk. paper)
ISBN-13 978-1-59038-617-0 (hardbound : alk. paper)
1. Paul, the Apostle, Saint. I. Title.
BS2506.3.W39 2006
225.9'2—dc22
[B] 2006010394

Printed in the United States of America
Worzalla Publishing Co., Stevens Point, WI

10 9 8 7 6 5 4 3 2 1

CONTENTS

ACKNOWLEDGMENTS

I would like to thank the great personnel at Deseret Book for bringing this project to fruition. I thank Cory Maxwell for his friendship, guidance, and support; Jay Parry, whose careful editorial work has made this book better; Shauna Gibby, the designer; Laurie Cook, the typesetter; and all those who worked on this project behind the scenes.

I would also like to thank the numerous friends and faculty members at Brigham Young University who have given insightful comments and conversations during the writing process.

My student assistants have been invaluable in collecting sources and tracking down important information. I would like to thank Nathan Justis, William Whitaker, Paul Lambert, and Jamie Karpowitz.

Above all others, I would like to thank Brandi, Shelby, and Cate for their understanding and encouragement along the way and for keeping me focused on completing this project.

CHRONOLOGY OF THE LIFE OF PAUL

Event	**Date**
Born	*c. A.D. 1**
Studies in Jerusalem under Gamaliel	*c. A.D. 20*
Returns to Tarsus	*mid A.D. 20s–32*
Stoning of Stephen in or near Jerusalem	*c. A.D. 32*
Experiences conversion on the road to Damascus	A.D. 32/33 (two years after the death of Jesus)
Visits Ananias and stays a short while in Damascus	A.D. 32/33
Flees Damascus; mission into Arabia	A.D. 33–35
Returns to Damascus, where he spends a brief time preaching the gospel	*c. A.D. 35*
Visits Jerusalem and speaks with Peter and James the Lord's brother	*c. A.D. 35*
Spends fourteen years in Syria-Cilicia, the region of his hometown	A.D. 35–49 (Paul's mission with Barnabas occurred at the end of this fourteen-year period)
Mission with Barnabas	A.D. 46–49
John Mark departs from Paul and Barnabas' company	*c. A.D. 47*
Attends the Jerusalem conference	A.D. 49
Departs on a mission without Barnabas	A.D. 49–52/53
Writes Galatians	c. A.D. 50
Eighteen-month stay in Corinth; writes 1 Thessalonians	Winter A.D. 50–51
Arrives in Ephesus; writes 2 Thessalonians	A.D. 52–53
Jerusalem visit	*c. A.D. 53*

**Dates that are based on conjecture are set in italics.*

Serves his final mission	c. A.D. 54–58
Stays in Ephesus and teaches at the school of Tyrannus. Paul is eventually imprisoned here, where he writes to Corinth and Philippi. He is later released.	A.D. 54–57
Returns to Corinth	A.D. 57
Writes 2 Corinthians and Romans after leaving Corinth	A.D. 57
Travels to Jerusalem to deliver the offering for the poor	c. A.D. 58
Imprisoned in Caesarea	Spring A.D. 58–60
Writes Ephesians, Colossians, and Philemon	While in prison at Caesarea
Travels by sea to Rome while under arrest; spends the winter months on the island of Malta.	Fall A.D. 60–Spring A.D. 61
Writes to the Hebrew saints	*While in prison at Rome*
Writes 1–2 Timothy and Titus while in Rome	A.D. 61–63
Death in Rome	c. A.D. 63

INTRODUCTION

Perhaps the most important reason for writing another historical biography of any individual from the past is that in seeing their lives more clearly we are able to appreciate our own lives more fully. The challenges of great individuals from the past become our own challenges in the present, and even though we may assume that we cannot see a way out of the current turmoil, the success of others can inspire us to try. When coupled with faith this process often leads to success in our own lives.

The apostle Paul remains to this day a largely enigmatic figure, a man whose name is intimately familiar, like the name of a great river; but like the river, whose beginning and ending are far distant, the portion that is in immediate view is quite cloudy. The segment of Paul's life with which we are familiar is limited to what we can see from the bank of the river, and even that view is quite murky on closer inspection.

This biography is not written from the standpoint of a new discovery, but from the perspective of appreciation of a hidden treasure, a treasure that has thus far remained hidden but certainly within reach. My own quest began to take shape when I had my first glimpse of understanding into the words of Paul.

For a brief moment, many years ago, Paul did not seem so intimidating. My initial efforts to learn more, however, were soon met with frustration as I realized that that short glimpse did not open the door wide enough to provide complete comprehension.

I read his letters again and again, and ultimately began studying the history and background of the communities to whom he wrote. This quest opened a door into the life of the apostle Paul, and subsequently a new series of insights began to appear before me. This part of the quest has been the most enduring, still occupying portions of my time on a regular basis.

Up to this point, my appreciation of Paul had been limited to a few insights into his character from personal study of his letters, alongside a rich accumulation of facts and details from the historical time period of Paul's life. I found many of the books on Paul fascinating and admired the great erudition of those who had written on the subject of Paul. I was impressed with their ability to handle such a difficult subject. What makes the subject even more difficult to master is that it can be known only through a series of letters that were never intended to provide a wealth of biographical detail.

The most meaningful portion of my quest came when I traveled to many of the cities of Paul's life, those that he had visited primarily in his second and third missionary journeys. Some may argue that at this point I was really experiencing a sense of fascination rather than appreciation, but from that point onward the life of Paul, his experiences, struggles, triumphs, passions, and character fell into place for me. He became real, tangible, almost a present reality, much like the Savior does in his visit to the Nephites.

At this stage in my understanding, it became apparent that emulation of those who had written on Paul previously was what I should pursue. A magnum opus, the "best" book ever written on Paul became my aspiration. Such attempts have been made, and many of these books are a true education between decorative cardboard covers. I began the book several times; and I continued to read with passion and vigor until I reached this current stage of thinking.

Academic books are written by scholars and for scholars, and once in a great while a scholarly book becomes popular and reaches a greater audience, although my skepticism has led me to believe that many of these books look better on the shelf than in the hands. I wanted others to experience what I have experienced, or at least find in my work a stepping-stone for their own quest and inquiry. Many, I am certain, have progressed farther along the path of understanding Paul, and therefore I would imagine that many other books will be written on this subject. I plan to read them all. The short list of the greatest and most important men and woman of all time must include the apostle Paul, for he laid the groundwork for the conversion of an empire. It is in appreciation of his life and ministry that I make this contribution.

Join with me in the quest to bring Paul to life for our families, to invite him into our lessons, and to help him in enlightening our personal understanding of, as Paul often referred to him, Lord Jesus.

Chapter 1

EARLY EXPERIENCES

" . . . the Apostle Paul, the greatest missionary the world has ever known . . ."
—Jeffrey R. Holland

Beneath the murky waters of Paul's early life runs a clear stream of experiences and ideas that shaped the life of the man who became perhaps Christianity's greatest missionary. Those experiences eventually ran together into a single confluence, but in his early days Paul's life can best be described as a succession of tiny rivulets, which formed to make small streams and brooks. Upon their entry into the larger stream of Paul's life, the water from these smaller streams continued to shape Paul's character in positive and powerful ways.

Paul's life is a primary example of how God shapes the individual for the desired task. Not all individuals travel through the same preparatory experiences, each of us needing specialized attention and care. In working with metals, heat renders them strong, giving them temper and rigidity, but too much heat renders them soft. Metals, especially tools used for cutting, can become too rigid, too hard, and therefore brittle, making them incapable of holding a sharp edge for more than a few hours of work. On the other hand, metal that has not been heated enough cannot be made to hold a sharpened edge and therefore is almost entirely useless as a cutting tool. Soft metal is malleable but impractical for long-term use.

In the forge of God, soft metals are heated and then appropriately molded into the desired tool, each piece of metal receiving the personal attention of the Master Craftsman. Most metals are heated and shaped repeatedly until they are perfectly formed, at which point they are thrust into cool water or oil, a process that completes the hardening of the metal. Slow cooling of the metal will not give it the desired temper.

Paul's tempering took place in a Jewish home, several hundred miles away from the Jewish homeland in a region that was relatively hospitable to Jewish immigrants but not dominated by a Jewish population or subculture. Tarsus, Paul's birthplace, is far enough from Jerusalem to be beyond the reaches of the Pharisaic and Sadduceean dynamics of Judea and Galilee, but close enough for members of a faithful Jewish family to maintain their emotional ties to their homeland.

The natural beauty of Tarsus, located at the base of the Taurus Mountains and a short distance from the Mediterranean coast, was conducive to a reflective attitude in its inhabitants but could have acted as a calming influence. One geographer described the idyllic setting of Paul's hometown by saying, "As for Tarsus, it lies in a plain; and it was founded by the Argives who wandered with Triptolemus in quest of Io; and it is intersected in the middle by the Cydnus River, which flows past the very gymnasium of the young men. Now inasmuch as the source of the river is not very far away and its stream passes through a deep ravine and then empties immediately into the city, its discharge is both cold and swift; and hence it is helpful both to men and to cattle that are suffering from swollen sinews, if they immerse themselves in its waters" (Strabo, *Geography,* 14.5.12).

The city boasted an impressive pedigree of famous visitors. Historians of the era record that the philosophers Athenodorus and Apollonius lived in the city together with the great statesman Cicero and the famous intellectual Nestor the Academic. In the middle of the first century B.C. it was graced with a visit by Marc Antony and Cleopatra when they sailed triumphantly up the river Cydnus. Tarsus, in the Roman period, was quickly becoming a haven for philosophers and intellectuals alike.

The fact that Jews could live in harmony with—or, perhaps more accurately, alongside—Gentiles in Tarsus was made possible through the relocation of Jews into the city and the surrounding regions after Antiochus IV Epiphanes (reigned 175–164 B.C.) reestablished the city in the middle of the second century B.C. Jewish settlers of the period took advantage of the opportunity to relocate to major population centers such as Ephesus, Antioch, and Alexandria or smaller cities such as Tarsus where they could find greater economic opportunities.

Since at least the eighth century B.C., Jews had been carried away captive to distant lands such as Assyria. In the sixth century, Babylon also captured Judea and led many of the inhabitants of Jerusalem into captivity. Those taken during the Assyrian and Babylonian conquest of the Holy Land were sometimes forcefully relocated, and at other times they were relocated peacefully into other cities of the Mediterranean basin. Later, under Roman rule, some voluntarily left their homeland to seek economic opportunities in foreign cities. Those Jews who relocated into other areas, such as Tarsus, quickly formed communities and built places of worship in those new cities. These scattered communities were later known as Diaspora Judaism, or scattered Judaism. They maintained their ethnic and religious identity, but because they did not live in Judea and her environs they were considered to be part of scattered Israel.

For a Jew living in a Diaspora community, certain regions of the Roman Empire were more hospitable than others to Jews and Jewish culture. Antiochus IV Epiphanes was not a friend of Jews, but his vision of a Hellenized Judea provided opportunities for geographic relocation among Jewish families. Even if they did not agree with the sometimes-forced secularization of their native religion under Antiochus, Jewish families could take advantage of the climate of acceptance and relocate throughout the empire. Tarsus, in the first century A.D., was a major commercial and intellectual center in the northeastern Mediterranean, and for Jewish families it was a fairly popular place for relocation because of the economic opportunities it provided and because of its proximity to their homeland.

SLAVERY

Paul's family most likely came to Tarsus as captives during one of the first-century Roman incursions into Galilee from Syria; indeed, this is the earliest surviving tradition about his origins and parentage. Jerome reports, "Paul, formerly called Saul, an apostle outside the number of the twelve apostles, was of the tribe of Benjamin and the town of Giscalis in Judea. When this was taken by the Romans he removed with his parents to Tarsus in Cilicia" (*Lives of Illustrious Men*, 5). Although Jerome here reports that Paul was carried away captive, the historical time frame suggests that it may have been Paul's grandparents who were taken into captivity. Therefore, Paul's parents would have been born into slavery, but not the type of chattel slavery etched in our memories from colonial America. Nevertheless, the condition of his parents or grandparents *was* slavery to a Roman master, who was most likely a former soldier who had been granted land in the regions around Syria.

Modern sympathies have tended to elevate the practice of slavery in Roman society, but one first-century observer noted, "we maltreat them, not as if they were men, but as if they were beasts of burden" (Seneca, *Epistle,* 47). Admittedly Seneca may have had in mind the mistreatment of slaves in the capital city, but, nonetheless, slavery of any sort dehumanizes an individual and creates a longing for freedom that cannot be appreciated under other circumstances.

Paul's ancestors were probably led away captive during Gabinius's invasion, which reached Mount Tabor in about 57 B.C. and which Josephus described saying, "But he [Gabinius] could not restrain Alexander, for he had an army of thirty thousand Jews, and met Gabinius, and, joining battle with him, was beaten, and lost ten thousand of his men about Mount Tabor" (*Antiquities,* 14.6.3). Some four years later, Cassius (c. 53 B.C.) captured Taricheae/Magdala, taking "thirty thousand Jews into slavery" (Josephus, *War,* 1.8.9). In either situation, the incursion of Gabinius or Cassius, Roman troops reached far enough into Galilee that Paul's ancestors could have been caught up in the resistance fighting or taken as part of the reparations for the losses experienced in war.

Both Roman incursions into Jewish territories met stiff Hasmonean resistance, and both took place nearly two generations before Paul's birth, thus presenting the distinct possibility that Paul's grandparents were carried into captivity but that his parents were manumitted or given their freedom according to Roman practice. Following Roman practice, the children of captured slaves would be released from slavery, thus opening the way for them to either purchase their citizenship or to receive it as a gift in return for meritorious service to Rome.

As slaves, Paul's family would have worked at a trade, providing income for their master, and at the same time were likely allowed to retain some of their earnings. This money could be used to meet the needs of the family or, eventually, to purchase freedom. Because of Paul's occupation as a "tentmaker" (Acts

18:3), the most likely scenario is that his family acquired this skill while in servitude and that Paul was taught to make canvas and tents at an early age.

Paul himself was free born. Still, his names "Saul" and "Paul" bear traces of a servile background. According to Roman practice in the first century, freed slaves were often distinguished by the name or nickname of the first person in their family to receive citizenship. Typically the patron or owner of the slave did not pass on his last name to his freedmen but allowed his freed slaves to retain the owner's first name or nicknames as a new family name. Therefore Paul likely descends from an ancestor named *Paulus,* meaning "short" or "stubby," a clear indication of a nickname given to a slave boy. Paul was brought into life in a family that knew servitude, but not necessarily hostile servitude. The name Saul is likely Paul's birth name, given in remembrance of the most famous member of the tribe of Benjamin, King Saul, who also fought to free Israel (1 Samuel 9–10).

The migration of Jewish families into Mediterranean societies under Antiochus would have provided a way for Jews who had been given their freedom to assimilate themselves back into the cultural mainstream. Paul's ancestors likely had continued contact with the Jewish community in Tarsus, and when his parents were granted their freedom they would have been able to maintain their residence in Tarsus and enjoy the friendships they had created there.

As former servants, Paul's ancestors, like other freed slaves, may have remained in close proximity to their former master, who could provide certain economic advantages. The practice of freed slaves working for their former masters was common in the first century. A former master could continue to offer work in the trade that the slave family had acquired during years of servitude in return for a small fee or share of the profits. Such close contact between the enslaved and freed is envisioned by Philo who recorded, "How then did he look upon the great division of Rome which is on the other side of the river Tiber, which he was well aware was occupied and inhabited by Jews? And they were mostly Roman citizens, having been emancipated; for, having been brought as captives into Italy, they were manumitted by those who had bought them for slaves, without ever having been compelled to alter any of their hereditary or national observances" (*On the Embassy to Gaius,* 23 §155). Much like Paul's ancestors, the Jews depicted in Philo's account were brought to the capital city as captives but were eventually granted their freedom. After receiving their freedom, the majority stayed in Rome to work because it had become a hospitable place for them to reside.

Freedom, the ultimate irony scorned by those who work to enhance the comfort and luxury of others, was an abstract ideal to Paul's ancestors. Teaching freedom through religion may have brought some solace to those who were forced to serve others, but genuine and true freedom could only remain abstract, something achieved through death and salvation through God. Freedom, whether release from physical responsibilities or true freedom of choice, must have become a focal point of family discussions, and in the heart of a young man bearing the common slave name "stubby" a burning desire to experience real freedom developed.

Servitude of any sort refines identity, not in a positive way, but in a way where it is accompanied by passion, disdain, and even hate. Those who are forced into serving others become acutely aware of who they are and what they could achieve if granted their freedom. These impulses, when combined with youth, can often lead to violent outbreaks, or destruction of the moral fiber so that achieving the desired end result—freedom—supercedes the restraints of conscience. Paul's passionate response to Christianity reveals a certain violence of character that in many ways is similar to someone who has been suppressed or in servitude. His violent outbreaks against Christians, whom Paul perceived to be heretics in his own religious tradition, is not typical of other Jews.

EDUCATION

In the socially diverse environment of first-century Tarsus, Paul the young man received at least the rudiments of a proper education. Characterizations of Tarsus in the first century glorify its atmosphere of learning: "The people at Tarsus have devoted themselves so eagerly, not only to philosophy, but also to the whole round of education in general, that they have surpassed Athens, Alexandria, or any other place that can be named where there have been schools and lectures of philosophers" (Strabo, *Geography*, 14.5.13).

As a young Jewish boy, Paul would have studied the law and the prophets with a teacher from the local synagogue who required his students to memorize portions of the scriptures, particularly excerpts from the five books of Moses. This type of training provided an easily recognizable means of differentiating between the abilities of students. The brightest students could show their skill and acumen by reciting large portions of scripture at a time, being the first among their peers to memorize the assigned passages, as well as to retain in memory earlier lessons.

Even today, this type of rote memorization can create an impression of superiority among those who are able to memorize quickly and accurately. Those who have memorized large amounts of material can often astound their audience by their sheer ability to recall large amounts of material without aid. But the ability to memorize does not necessarily demonstrate critical thinking skills.

Whether education through memorization is a good measure of proficiency is subjective, but in the Jewish and also Greco-Roman way of thinking, memorization was one of the first steps in a proper education.

After a sufficient body of material had been memorized—in the case of a Jewish youth portions of the five books of Moses (the Torah) and the Psalms, or in the case of a Greek or Roman youth portions of Homer or the great orators—the teacher moved on to the practice of emulation and the early development of critical thinking skills. In Greco-Roman society, students were required to copy the style, vocabulary, and diction of an assigned author. Proficiency was measured through the students' ability to imitate an author. The practice of memorizing and imitating an author inadvertently led to a certain appreciation for that author. The educational system, in fact, was partially built on the foundational concept that imitation is the greatest form of flattery.

Paul would have moved from the process of memorization to lessons in critical thinking. Jewish youth were often given a dilemma to ponder and then asked to draw on the body of material they had memorized, as well as other scriptures, to provide an answer. In this manner, students could deal with apparent contradictions in a faithful atmosphere where the ultimate answers always originated in the word of God.

Paul's later epistles reveal that he had received some level of training in both Jewish and Greco-Roman traditions. He was obviously better versed in Jewish scriptures, particularly the Greek translation of the Hebrew Old Testament (the Septuagint), but there is also a consistent level of appreciation for and demonstration of Greco-Roman forms of thinking and expression. During Paul's speech on Mars Hill, or the Hill of Ares, he cited, possibly from memory, the works of the sixth-century poet Epimenides, "For in him we live, and move, and have our being," and the work of Aratus, a third-century Attic poet, "For we are also his offspring" (Acts 17:28; *Phaenomena*, 5).

GROWING UP BILINGUAL

Later in life, Paul, in his epistles, fortunately preserved some of his pre-Christian attitudes concerning his abilities as a student of the law and regarding his own righteousness. In one of his latest epistles—Philippians—Paul refers to his early training, saying, "If any other man thinketh that he hath whereof he might trust in the flesh, I more: Circumcised the eighth day, of the stock of Israel, of the tribe of Benjamin, an Hebrew of the Hebrews; as touching the law, a Pharisee; concerning zeal, persecuting the church; touching the righteousness which is in the law, blameless" (Philippians 3:4–6). Paul, by ridiculing his opponents' claims to superiority, provides a glimpse into his own prior feelings of superiority.

According to his own words, the early Paul felt that he was "blameless" and that he had more trust in his own abilities or in his own "flesh" than did anyone else. As a Christian, Paul later realized the foolishness of such thinking, saying, "doubtless . . . I count all things but loss for the excellency of the knowledge of Christ Jesus my Lord" (Philippians 3:8). Such pride and overconfidence in one's own abilities reveals an early life of intellectual success and ardent pursuit of religious ideals. In this instance, the future disciple's early accomplishments, when coupled with an increasing religious zeal, led to the false impression that ascendancy in some areas meant superiority in others.

Singular greatness, or remarkable achievement in a single field, has a surprisingly small surface area when compared with the structure that some try to build upon it. It is not uncommon to assume that excellence in one area will certainly lead to excellence in others. From Paul's own words, he seems to have built upon a substructure consisting of his own glorious lineage "of the stock of Israel, of the tribe of Benjamin, an Hebrew of the Hebrews" that in turn led him to believe that he was "blameless" (Philippians 3:4–6). The pride inherent in Paul's assumption that his commendable lineage translated into exceptional character led to a fall, one that would bring him low enough to realize that the original surface area of his character was insufficient to support the demanding structure of a disciple's life.

Every indication from Paul points to the fact that he excelled in his studies and that pride in his Jewish training led to overconfidence. Accounting for Paul's completely intolerant attitudes toward Christians is something that forces a closer look at his early development. Not all Jews hated Christians, nor could one say that even a majority of Jews hated Christians. The Gospels portray Jewish hatred of Jesus and his disciples as originating from a small faction of the ruling elite, and indicate that generally the crowds acted favorably towards Jesus.

Paul, however, developed such an intolerance of Christians that he propelled himself to the front line of the offensive, a strategy intended to eradicate the followers of Jesus from among the ranks of faithful Jews. Some of Paul's fanaticism was born of his own scholastic superiority and mental prowess, but such cerebral athleticism can account for only a portion of the driving force that would lead him to seek the complete eradication of Christians or Christianity.

FURTHER STUDY IN JERUSALEM

Sometime in his later teens, perhaps even as late as his early twenties, Paul left Tarsus to pursue further educational opportunities in Jerusalem. Paul probably brought with him an attitude of superiority, a result of early successes and comparatively greater abilities than his peers. Jerusalem was the logical place to pursue further study; Tarsus had offered him all of her secular academic training, but any serious student of the law needed to pursue study under one of the great Jewish teachers of the day.

For a young Diaspora Jewish family, the social dynamics of the sectarian debates between Pharisees and Sadducees must have seemed distant and removed from their environment or immediate concern. Those outside of Jerusalem were aware of the differences between Pharisees and Sadducees, but sympathy for either group was the result of a conscious decision rather than the culturally mandated decision it had become in Judea. Moreover, the Pharisees offered clear and practical answers to life's real issues, thus making them the preferred choice of the masses, as well as among Diaspora families. The Sadducees represented the ruling aristocratic land class, who taught that revelation had ended with Moses and also that mankind ceased to exist with death, answers that offered very little hope to a people who prayed and hoped that their present obedience would yield some tangible blessing in the hereafter.

Relocating to Jerusalem represented more than a physical change in scenery. In reality Judea, and Jerusalem in particular, invited young and bright scholars to enter into the world of divided sectarian Judaism. It was a chance for promising students to further differentiate themselves from their peers. The family who remained at home must have made great sacrifices, not only sparing their sons for years of training but also losing any potential income. No serious student of the law, however, could afford to pass up such an opportunity.

Tarsus, a beautiful city in its own right, could not compare to the splendor of Jerusalem when her temple was still standing. Not only was Jerusalem striking, but also her spiritual importance inspired greater appreciation of her natural beauty. Paul, possibly leaving his parents behind, traveled to the Jewish homeland, the very center of his spiritual world. In the words of one first-century commentator, the city had become "the site of peace," the embodiment of peace (Philo, *On Dreams*, 2.38 §250). Another later Jewish intellectual lamented that in Jerusalem's splendor, when the temple was standing, "Ten qabs [measures] of beauty came down into the world, nine were taken by Jerusalem, and one by the rest of the entire world" (Bavli Qiddushin, 2:2). In Paul's day, with the temple still standing, Jerusalem still possessed her nine measures of beauty.

To go to Jerusalem was to come home. In traveling the dusty road through Jericho, or the sometimes-dangerous Samaritan road, one literally ascends into Jerusalem. The city can be spotted from a distance, and the glorious Herodian Temple must have seemed like a jewel amid the palms. With each step closer to Jerusalem, Paul would have experienced the sights, smells, and familiarity of his own home in a wider cultural setting. Paul's home in Tarsus was one of many tiny oases in the midst of a Greco-Roman influenced society, whereas he was now in the midst of his countrymen, fully engulfed in the spiritual oasis of Jewish life and culture.

GAMALIEL

Whether Paul sought out a great teacher prior to arriving in Jerusalem is unknown. Among the notable first-century teachers living at the time of Paul were the successors of the schools of Hillel and Shammai. The two great Pharisaic teachers had become so influential in the intellectual environment of first-century Judea that their opinions, or the opinions of their later disciples, were sought in almost all important matters. Several of Jesus' preserved teachings reveal an intimate knowledge of the doctrinal debates going on between the two teachers. In one instance, Jesus' teachings on marriage and divorce, the statement that a man can divorce for any reason at all (Matthew 19:3), is clearly a proposition set forth by the more liberal school of Hillel, while the more conservative school of Shammai held that divorces should be granted only in cases of fornication. For example, the school of Shammai is reported as teaching, "The House of Shammai say, 'A man should divorce his wife only because he has found grounds for it in unchastity,' since it is said, 'Because he has found in her indecency in anything' (Deut. 24:1). And the House of Hillel say, 'Even if she spoiled his dish,' since it is said, 'Because he has found in her indecency in anything'" (Bavli Gittin, 9:10). Although filled with anti-Hillel rhetoric, this passage preserves the core issues of the debate between the two predominant Pharisaic first-century schools of thought.

The semi-liberal positions taken by Hillel and his later pupils seem to have provided an ill fit for Paul and other neo-conservative Jewish youth. In fact, the staunch conservatism taught by John the Baptist was likely closer to Paul's own positions than any other Jewish teacher known to be active in Jerusalem during Paul's day. However, when faced with the choice of whether to follow the school of Shammai or Hillel, Paul chose to study under Gamaliel, the grandson and successor of the school of Hillel. In some ways, Paul might have found a more intellectually familiar environment in the school of Shammai, but for some reason he did not study under him. It is important to note, however, that no evidence exists suggesting that Paul came to Jerusalem with ultraconservative views on religious purity, but instead his religious radicalism seems to have blossomed in Jerusalem. He may have felt, prior to his time in Jerusalem, that his viewpoints were more liberal than they really were, whereas his schooling revealed the more conservative tendencies in his character (Romans 7:9).

Of Gamaliel, the Mishnah records, "When Rabban Gamaliel the Elder died, the glory of the Law ceased and purity and abstinence died" (Sotah, 49b). Later reports demonstrate that the school of Gamaliel focused on the issue of sexual purity, teaching that husbands, contrary to common practice, could not annul their marriages without the consent of their wives (Bavli Gittin, 4:2); although his successors became more lax on the issue of divorce specifically. This continued focus on purity represents a consistent thread in the discussions at the school. Paul, for whatever reasons, was drawn to this school of thought, and would have been trained in the tradition of Hillel that the purity of Judaism had been compromised through improper Sabbath observance and marriage customs. He was known for over a hundred years after his death as a defender of "purity and abstinence."

The theme of purity within Judaism expounded at the school of Hillel struck a cord in the young Pharisee from Tarsus, who learned that his faith was internally polluted through misguided obedience and practice. If Paul applied the principles of the school of Gamaliel, then the result would be an attitude of strict reform and correction. However, the New Testament records that Gamaliel himself was moderate in his attitudes towards Christians and other supposed heretics. Acts records a portion of Gamaliel's words to the Sanhedrin: "For before these days rose up Theudas, boasting himself to be somebody; to whom a number of men, about four hundred, joined themselves: who was slain; and all, as many as obeyed him, were scattered, and brought to nought. . . . And now I say unto you, Refrain from these men, and let them alone: for if this counsel or this work be of men, it will come to nought: But if it be of God, ye cannot overthrow it; lest haply ye be found even to fight against God" (Acts 5:36–39). Gamaliel provided a logical framework for a radical reformation within Judaism focused on purity, yet he was a liberal in application and practiced restraint in his dealings with Christians and others he felt were misguided.

Paul probably recognized the implications of Gamaliel's tolerant attitudes; however, as the passions of youth began to blossom and the feelings of superiority began to manifest themselves, Paul moved in a direction away from his teacher. Paul never mentioned his training under Gamaliel, but at some time privately conveyed the information to Luke or Luke's sources. Paul's silence about his training under Gamaliel may imply a level of embarrassment that the moderate attitudes of his teacher proved to be more correct than the recalcitrant and reactionary attitudes adopted by Paul himself.

One early tradition may preserve some historical reference to Paul's eventual split with Gamaliel. It records, "Whoever forgets the basic principle of the Sabbath and performs many acts of labor on many different Sabbath days is liable only for a single sin-offering. He who knows the principle of the Sabbath and performs many acts of labor on many different Sabbaths is liable for the violation of each and every Sabbath: *Both Rab and Samuel say, 'Our Mishnah paragraph speaks of a child who was kidnapped by gentiles or a proselyte who converted while living among gentiles,* but if one originally knew about the Sabbath but in the end forgot about it, one is liable for violation of each and every Sabbath'" (Shabbath, 68b; emphasis added). Although the tradition does not specifically mention Paul, it does speak of one who knew the law and then forgot it. A further reference is made to a conversion (kidnapping) to gentile ways, which probably is in reference to Paul, who knew the law but then converted to what the source equates as gentile ways.

Whether Paul returned to Tarsus following his schooling in Jerusalem or immediately began to persecute Christians is unclear, but Paul almost certainly quit studying under Gamaliel prior to his departure for Damascus. His earlier attitudes of superiority could not be kept in check through a policy of temperance, and Paul likely felt himself intellectually superior to his teachers. The logical corollary to Gamaliel's teachings was zealous reform, and Paul, unlike his teacher, was willing to act against impurity.

THE UNKNOWN YEARS

Paul's life after his departure from Jerusalem and before his reappearance in Jerusalem at the stoning of Stephen (Acts 8:1) is almost impossible to trace. A few hints may shed some light on his whereabouts and doings, but they must remain hints and not facts. As a young adult in a Jewish society, Paul would likely have married in his mid to late teens. No evidence from Paul's early life hints that he was not married, although after his conversion there is no evidence that he was married. One later tradition, which may preserve some historical kernel of truth, reports, "They declare that he was a Greek. . . . He went up to Jerusalem, they say, and when he had spent some time there, he was seized with a passion to marry the daughter of the priest. For this reason he became a proselyte (through the Sadducee movement, hence his working for the temple police) and was circumcised. Then, when he failed to get the girl, he flew into a rage and wrote against circumcision and against the Sabbath and the Law" (Epiphanius, *Panarion,* 30:16–19).

Like the book of Acts, this quotation preserves a tradition that Paul studied in Jerusalem, but unlike Acts, it reports that Paul converted to the Sadduceean school of thought. His supposed change in outlook came as a result of an infatuation he developed with the high priest's daughter, who spurned his advances, thus causing Paul to leave his ancestral faith and become a Christian. Epiphanius's report, which probably originates from an anti-Christian Jewish source, is an obvious attempt to explain why Paul converted to Christianity, saying it was not a genuine, heartfelt conversion but rather an attempt to strike at the faith of a girl who had turned him away. What fits well with the historical account preserved by Luke is that Paul was in Jerusalem at about the age when he should have been married and that he may have fallen in love with the daughter of one of the prominent members of the Sanhedrin, perhaps the daughter of the high priest.

Paul's letters, written when he was in his forties and fifties, show someone who was familiar with family dynamics, particularly the bonds between husbands and wives (1 Corinthians 7:4–5). Therefore, the most plausible solution, given such fragmentary evidence, is that Paul was married but that his wife had passed away before they had children and prior to the time when Paul began his second missionary journey into Asia and Greece.

If this is the case, it may reveal one more facet of why Paul acted so forcefully against Christians. Assuming that Paul was nearly as old as Jesus' disciples, and therefore near thirty years old at his conversion, then he likely experienced not only the blossoming of his vanity at an early age, but also the extreme emotional trauma of losing a spouse (or as Epiphanius's apocryphal source implies, the pain experienced in being turned down).

Paul's experiences prior to his conversion created a philosophical foundation for his persecution of Christianity, and when coupled with a youthful sense of superior intelligence, paved the way for a moderate Pharisee to become a reactionary persecutor. But such a foundation needed a spark to ignite it. It is possible that the loss of his spouse would have generated sufficient feelings of detachment and despair that he sought to transfer his internal misery to his external surroundings.

Those who lose a child or a spouse react in numerous ways, often in a positive way that brings them closer to Christ and to the hope that they will see their loved ones again. On the other hand, some turn against God because in their perception he allowed such an awful thing to happen to them. Sometimes a death is seen as an unfair or insurmountable trial. Paul seems to have reacted more in line with those who turn to God, choosing to dedicate his life and energy to the pursuit of purity within his own religion. His new hyper-religious attitude surfaced shortly before Stephen appeared in the synagogue of the Libertines in Jerusalem.

During the years immediately before his conversion to Christianity, Paul also returned to Jerusalem. After having studied under Gamaliel, it seems likely that Paul returned to his family in Tarsus. Paul's later epistles do not betray an intimate knowledge of Judea-Palestine, and although he had certainly visited Jerusalem, it is not clear that he had spent a significant amount of time there. Therefore, the natural conclusion is that Paul probably traveled to Tarsus and remained there with his family, working at a trade and perfecting his skills as a tentmaker.

Politically, the years between A.D. 30 and 32, the likely timeframe of Paul's conversion, were relatively peaceful in the eastern Mediterranean, although Pilate's governorship in Judea was beginning to deteriorate. However, in Caesarea, Pilate "introduced Caesar's effigies, which were upon the ensigns, and brought them into the city; whereas our law forbids us the very making of images" (Josephus, *Antiquities*, 18.3.1). Naturally the devout citizenry were revolted at such a pagan incursion into their city, being offended particularly at Pilate's lack of consideration for their beliefs. Pilate threatened the Jews of the city with death if they inhibited his actions, which threat caused the Jews to throw "themselves upon the ground, and laid their necks bare, and said they would take their death very willingly, rather than the wisdom of their laws should be transgressed" (Josephus, *Antiquities*, 18.3.1). Pilate relented, but the event shed a pall over Pilate's governorship and caused Jews to distrust him and his motives.

Not long after, in A.D. 36, Pilate received news that the Samaritans were assembling on Mount Gerezim in honor of a local demagogue. To circumvent any political uprising, Pilate sent troops there to block their ascent up the mount. Pilate was able to keep the Samaritans from ascending the mount; he then executed the ringleaders and "most potent" participants (Josephus, *Antiquities,* 18.4.1). The Samaritans reported Pilate to Vitellius, the governor of Syria, who then ordered Pilate to return to Rome to answer the charges (Josephus, *Antiquities,* 18.4.2). Pilate's actions in the period of A.D. 30 to 36 led local Jews and Samaritans to distrust him, but also, as the two examples from the time period demonstrate, they began to generate a popular resistance movement.

The second century B.C. zealots, whose revolts against foreign oppression had been tempered somewhat in the years before Jesus' birth, began to surface anew. Rather than suffer idolatrous images to enter their cities, some Jews willingly laid down their lives. Paul, like many of his Jewish countrymen, may have returned to Judea-Galilee for the very same reasons that caused these Jewish men to offer their own lives in sacrifice. The purity of their nation and religion was of greater importance than physical longevity. Paul, in Acts, appears in Jerusalem during the same time period that these events transpired. He is also associated with a radical group of Jews who had designated Christians as another source of impurity. This group openly opposed Christianity and was willing, on trumped-up charges of blasphemy, to take the lives of those who taught that Jesus was the Christ.

Chapter 2

THE GROWTH OF THE EARLY CHURCH

"It is well for us to remember as far as we know that Paul took no part in making the decision that condemned Stephen and fortunately took no part in the stoning which cost Stephen his life. That he was in full sympathy with what was done we may well believe. . . . It is likely true that he sanctioned the action."
—Joseph Fielding Smith

The first years of growth for the Christian church must have caught the attention of those who thought they had won a great victory with the death of Jesus of Nazareth. Between the death of Jesus in A.D. 30 and the conversion of Paul in c. A.D. 32, the early church had made an open and provocative statement of faith. As Luke begins the story in Acts, after many of the followers of Jesus had fled Jerusalem to avoid capture at his arrest, a significant group of Christians gathered once again in Jerusalem to proclaim Jesus as Lord. The book of Acts begins with a private meeting of disciples on the Mount of Olives, where the Lord appeared to them to give them further instruction for the establishment of the kingdom of God on earth. At that time the disciples appear to have been pondering the scope and extent of their missionary work and whether it would involve the restoration of the house of Israel, which at that time was quite fractured. Jesus made it clear to them that their mission would start in Jerusalem, extend into Samaria, and then go throughout the world (Acts 1:8). After the unjust and agonizing death of Jesus on the cross outside the city walls, the earliest apostles seem initially to have remained mostly behind closed doors, concerned that it was not yet safe to venture beyond their sanctuary in Jerusalem. In those early years after the arrest and crucifixion of Jesus, the apostles, particularly Peter, were wanted men and fugitives.

Not much more than fifty days after the death of Jesus outside the city walls of Jerusalem, the young leaders of the Christian church held a conference in the Holy City. They gathered on the day of Pentecost to declare that Jesus had been exalted in heaven and had taken his place at God's right hand (Acts 2:24–25, 36). Acts has preserved some of the initial shock of that day, where the disciples declared openly in front of devout Jews that the crucified Jesus had become both Lord and Messiah. Any reservations that the disciples felt about making their whereabouts known must have quickly vanished on that day. On that day, the first day of the Pentecost, the Lord demonstrated through divine manifestations that the apostles were indeed his servants. This was their first recorded public appearance to a crowd, where they ran the risk of being apprehended, beaten, or ignored.

The composition of the audience held special significance, for many of them appear to have been foreigners. Luke, who was probably not a member during these early months of the church, may have conflated two different gatherings that took place on that day. The first gathering consisted of a group of foreigners who had come to Jerusalem to celebrate the Pentecost (Acts 2:9–11). A second gathering may be suggested in Acts 2:14 by the fact that Peter is now speaking to the "men of

Judea," rather than the gathering of foreigners. Or there may simply have been only one gathering, which included many men of Judea as well as foreigners. In either case the disciples, now slightly more confident, spoke to those Jews whom they felt were responsible for the death of Jesus. The tone of their speech indicates that they were more certain of their footing, clearer in purpose, and ready to defend the faith independent of its Jewish origins.

Their testimony centered on the issue of Jesus and not on the law of Moses. Many have felt that Christians initially taught against the law of Moses in the early days of the church and that those teachings led to the break between Jews and Christians. Luke, however, does not record any disputes over the law of Moses until after the day of Pentecost, but instead points to the exaltation of Christ as the focal point of the new Christian faith. Surely many of Jesus' teachings were starting to make sense to the apostles after the resurrection had put them into perspective (John 2:22), but the reality of the exalted Christ still remained the central element in their testimonies.

Issues with the Law would certainly arise, eventually leading to a schism within the church itself, but in those early days when the apostles were finding their footing, they taught the resurrected Christ and that he was the fulfillment of scripture. Their teachings reveal a newness and spirit of scriptural inquiry. They had only the Old Testament, and each of them had surely grown up being taught the prophecies and teachings of scripture. For the early apostles, there must have been contradictions between what the Jews had taught regarding the coming of the Messiah and the now-unraveling doctrines of the first and second coming of the Savior. One contradiction that may have been particularly troubling was the teaching that anyone who was hung on a tree was accursed of God (Deuteronomy 21:23;

Galatians 3:13). Now they had to teach a crucified Messiah using those same scriptures.

As the early brethren continued to teach and preach in Jerusalem, there began to be a growing opposition to their testimony. For at least the first two or three years after Christ's resurrection, the apostolic ministry must have remained close to Jerusalem. The eleven apostles were farmers, fishermen, and simple people who spoke Aramaic and who may have been moderately familiar with Greek. From the day of Pentecost until the stoning of Stephen, there is no mention of any missionary activity outside of Jerusalem. The church was small even though multitudes were now joining it. The newly appointed apostles were faced with the demands of organizing and governing the church. They faced domestic disputes over the law of consecration (Acts 5:1–10), they taught the gospel openly (Acts 3:12–26; 4:8–12), and they tended to the temporal welfare of the saints (Acts 6:1–4). Jerusalem was the center of the church, and it was also the place where they expected the Lord to return. Many of the adversarial relationships that developed during Jesus' ministry were carried over into the early years of the church, when the apostles and believers were also persecuted and hindered (Acts 4:1–3; 5:17–18). Although the Lord had instructed the eleven to teach the gospel in Galilee and beyond, the opportunity to do so had not yet made itself manifest (Matthew 28:16–20). For the first few years, then, the church focused its attention on organization and preaching the gospel in the regions of Jesus' ministry—particularly Jerusalem.

Some months before the two-year anniversary of the post-resurrection church, a remarkable event took place that would open the doors for the gospel to be preached beyond Judea. We know that the apostles remained close to the synagogues in Jerusalem and taught there when occasion permitted. Luke records that in Jerusalem one particular synagogue was frequented by Diaspora Jews, Greeks, Alexandrians, and other foreigners who allowed Stephen to speak to them. In that synagogue, services would have been delivered in Greek. Stephen's preaching in that synagogue evoked a particularly passionate response, one that led to his death.

Luke was unaware of, or left unstated, Stephen's relationship with the synagogue of the Libertines. The term Libertines denotes a social status and is not an ethnic term. A Libertine was a freedman or a former slave who had won or purchased his freedom; therefore, the synagogue of the Libertines was the location where Greek-speaking former slaves met to hear the law of Moses taught to them in their own language. They were devout believers, but many of them, like Paul, had been raised in cities outside of Judea and were therefore less familiar with Aramaic or Hebrew—the common languages of the Judean synagogues. Stephen, who may have been a member or visiting member of the synagogue of the Libertines, taught something among them that they found deeply unsettling and distasteful.

Noted among the members of the synagogue were the "Cilicians," the regional designation of Paul's homeland. Luke may have included this story because of its direct connection with the apostle Paul. If indeed Paul was a citizen of Tarsus and had received Roman citizenship through his father, he might have felt right at home in this synagogue where freedmen and Greek-speaking Jews met to discuss the law of Moses. His first direct encounter with the church may have come when Stephen taught those of that synagogue the gospel. Stephen's speech raised a new concern among the opponents of Christianity—whether or not the teachings of Jesus of Nazareth contradicted the teachings of the law of Moses. For a young devout Jew such as Paul, teaching against the Law and that Jesus had become Deity could be viewed as nothing less than blasphemous. Luke introduces for the first time the issue of the law of Moses as a point of friction between Jews and Christians. Up to that point the tension had come over the claims of Christ's divinity.

If we assume that Paul was present the day of Stephen's speech, or that he had heard of it through contacts who attended the synagogue of the Libertines, we have an important causal link that would explain how Paul was enticed into the battle with these new followers of Jesus of Nazareth. A devout monotheist and follower of the law of Moses, Paul would have been offended by Stephen's teachings and would have felt duty bound to impede this new religious movement.

PAUL BECOMES A PERSECUTOR

Paul provides no clues in his personal writings to suggest that he, a new Pharisaic scribe, was searching or questioning his religious upbringing. Paul was not looking beyond Judaism for something more tangible, heartfelt, or personal. His beliefs were firmly anchored in the God of the Old Testament, and Paul viewed himself as an emissary of God.

Strong devotion, however, does not typically lead to persecution of outsiders and other religious movements. In the climate of Paul's day, Pharisees and Sadducees had coexisted for nearly two centuries. While Pharisaic persecution of Sadducees, and vice versa, is certainly noted in historical accounts from the period, there was a general attitude of tolerance between these two main religious sects, even if they felt the other group was inherently misguided. Josephus paints a vivid picture of the strained but relatively peaceful relationship that existed between Pharisees and Sadducees of the first century: "Great disputes and differences have arisen among them, while the Sadducees are able to persuade none but the rich, and have not the populace obsequious to them, but the Pharisees have the multitude on their side" (*Antiquities,* 13.10.6). Josephus's

Pharisaic leanings are evident in the quotation, but he nonetheless notes that differences in audience and teachings existed between the two groups.

Paul, being a Pharisee, must have been willing to tolerate what he perceived to be misinterpretations of scripture by the Sadducees. There are no accounts of Paul pursuing Sadducees or any other Jewish sectarian groups. Why, then, was Paul's position toward this newly emerging Jewish-Christian sect so extreme?

The dynamics of persecution literature and movements often reveal that the founding members of the group felt a need to settle a personal grudge or bias. Such origins may not be openly acknowledged, but often the impetus to begin persecution is closely related to a personal offense given by the person or group who is subsequently persecuted. This is clearly the situation in the Book of Mormon, where the descendants of Laman and Lemuel are taught to continue the hatred of their fathers, who took personal offense at their younger brother Nephi. Nearly four hundred and fifty years later, the descendants of Laman and Lemuel still complain that "they were wronged in the wilderness by their brethren, and they were also wronged while crossing the sea; and again, that they were wronged while in the land of their first inheritance, after they had crossed the sea" (Mosiah 10:12–13).

It often takes a significant personal offense for the ordinary member of society to step beyond the boundaries of acceptable behavior. While the differences between those who persecute and those who do not persecute may not be vast in all societies, compelling hate, distrust, or threat must be perceived in order to force normal citizens to go beyond the boundaries of civilized behavior and enter into the arena of persecution.

Family disputes are also another leading cause of intense persecution or hatred. Often, because family relationships are initially more intimate than normal societal relationships, family feuds lead to greater hatred and vengeance, which in turn can lead to ostracizing, neglect, and even persecution. The reasons for these actions are likely as numerous as the number of families in which they occur; yet family feuds are at the origin of some of society's fiercest battles. In a cosmic sense, this drama may be seen in the continuing hatred harbored by one of God's own sons. Most persecutors would have lost interest or momentum after thousands of years of persecution; however, Satan and his followers only appear to gain momentum and interest in the battle. Family battles of this sort must often be resolved through separation and distancing of the offended parties.

Another type of persecution that involves a similar level of hatred and vehemence is that generated through religious bigotry. An extensive study on the dynamics of religious hatred and persecution would likely fail to appreciate all of its nuances. Religious hatred has motivated the armies of nations, cost the lives of thousands, and toppled great governments and societies. At the core of religious persecution may be the sentiment that the views of the persecuted have raised doubts among those who persecute.

Often, those who persecute seek to vehemently deny or suppress other religious sentiments when they conflict directly with their own. When the beliefs of outsiders offer no compelling challenge, it is acceptable to permit those beliefs and believers to coexist side-by-side. If, however, the beliefs of outsiders offer a substantial threat to core doctrines and beliefs, then a sufficient impetus exists to overstep the bounds of civilized society and persecute those who hold such beliefs. This circumstance is often seen with new religious movements that challenge the norms of society and threaten to rethink the popular conceptions of that society. This was likely one of the primary reasons early Latter-day Saint communities were the object of such focused and severe persecution. Active and sustained missionary activity can also be interpreted as a hostile act in such an environment because it threatens to create more believers, thereby putting more pressure to act upon those who might otherwise respond passively toward the new religious movement.

Paul's zeal for his own religion got in the way of the agency of others. Unfortunately, the origins of Paul's religious bigotry and persecution have now been almost entirely lost to us. Paul never mentions why he hated Christians. Could he have resented the conversion of those close to him—even a close family member? Did he receive some offense from an early member of the church? Did Christianity threaten Paul's views, or did he feel that the Christian message presented a formidable obstacle to Jewish faith? Unfortunately, we cannot answer these questions with complete accuracy; although the few hints left to us by the apostle suggest that it had something to do with his own strong religious convictions and his own vaunted feelings of self-worth and pride in his own abilities.

In reflecting on his own pre-Christian past, Paul offers a glimpse into his own understanding of righteousness within the law of Moses. Paul's sentiments are construed as a superlative evaluation of his religious upbringing and standing. In Philippians 3:4–5, as noted before, Paul taught, "If any other man thinketh that he hath whereof he might trust in the flesh, I more: Circumcised the eighth day, of the stock of Israel, of the tribe of Benjamin, an Hebrew of the Hebrews." Although stated in opposition to opponents in Philippi, and with a hint of irony, the sense of comparison in the verse yields the understanding that Paul wants us to understand that he was a perfect, unspotted example of Jewish practice and heritage. The statement, made in the context of undermining the position of his enemies, would be analogous to the statement, "no one is a better Jew than I am, both by upbringing and by practice." Paul clearly did not think it prideful to call himself perfect or blameless.

Paul concludes by saying that he was, "blameless" according to the Law (Philippians 3:6). Although this type of religious sentiment might appear boastful or prideful when taken from its ancient context, it was appropriate for the religion of his day. Paul is not telling his audience that he had no need for redemption or repentance, but that by his interpretation of the law of Moses he could be considered clean. The requirements of the Law declared Paul clean, a claim that is informed by virtue of the Law's detailed description of what was righteousness and what was not. Paul's statement may, however, retain a slight hint of presumptuousness, although a later statement in Timothy seems to contradict it, saying that Paul thought himself to be the foremost among sinners (1 Timothy 1:15). Paul was not inconsistent in his attitudes. Paul could be both righteous according to the requirements of the Law, and yet after his conversion he realized that his pre-Christian righteousness amounted to little or nothing without faith in Jesus. Therefore, he can clearly state that he believed himself to be blameless only to learn later in life that his blamelessness was called into question with the atonement of Christ.

Paul's personality required that he do everything completely and give 100 percent. For Paul there was no way to be a fence-sitter and still be a believer; he felt one must literally take an all or nothing position. Paul could not be a part-time Jew, or partially committed in his devotion to Deity. He committed himself entirely and worked, with emphasis on *work*, toward becoming perfect before God. That attitude of perfection led him to believe that Judaism needed to be cleansed of its heretics and that the peaceful existence of Christians alongside Judaism threatened the purity of Paul's native religion. This attitude of intolerance is evident in another late first-century document often referred to as "the proscription against heretics." The document contains eighteen "blessings" or rules by which the synagogues should be governed. One of the so-called blessings is actually a condemnation of Christians who are referred to as "Nazarim" or "Nazarenes." The document condemns the supposedly apostate Christians by recommending that they be excommunicated from the synagogues, while at the same time invoking God to curse them for their apostasy.

Complacency toward a schism in the church can also be viewed as acceptance, and Paul's position against the growing Christian church reveals an inner commitment not to allow quiet acceptance to infringe upon his personal righteousness. If they were right, then Paul was wrong; but if Paul was right, they could not be tolerated. Paul's attitude and strong personal commitment to what he believed was right never changed after his conversion; he became an absolutely devoted follower of Christ. As early as his first epistle to the Thessalonians Paul congratulated the saints because they "became followers of us" (1 Thessalonians 1:6). Paul's pre-Christian blamelessness had now been transformed into Christian forgiveness, and Paul could speak of himself as an example worthy of emulation. Paul taught the Corinthians that they should seek to be "blameless in the day of our Lord Jesus Christ" (1 Corinthians 1:8). Paul in this instance speaks as one who has tasted blamelessness and wants to share how he had achieved this state of blamelessness.

Few among us will ever experience such confidence in the faith, many of us being worried that overconfidence infringes upon humility. Humility, however, does not demand weakness; instead, humility is proportionate to faith and good works, which in turn generate confidence in prayer and in the presence of the Lord. The greater confidence we have in our position before the Lord, the more humility becomes a choice instead of an attitude derived from circumstance. Paul was very confident. Perhaps he realized that Christianity needed a new set of heroes and models of faith, but perhaps he also had confidence from his personal relationship with God, which had begun when he was a Pharisaic scribe and had later blossomed under the gospel of Jesus Christ. Paul, on several important occasions, would prove to be a very humble servant.

THE STONING OF STEPHEN

By all accounts, Stephen was the first martyr of the Christian church. His testimony and stoning represent an important transition in church history and ironically helped to open doors for the gospel among Diaspora Jews and eventually Gentiles. The initial reaction against Stephen took place in the synagogue of the Libertines and, according to Luke, a mob of Jews took action against him for what he had taught. Luke has apparently interwoven two different threads of involvement into the account of the stoning of Stephen. The account begins with the "high priest" interrogating Stephen and ends with an act of unrestrained mob violence, thus indicating that Stephen's death was probably not an official act of the Sanhedrin. From the evidence left by Luke, the stoning of Stephen was carried out in heated anger against a Christian missionary who had offended Jewish sensibilities.

Luke's account of the story seems to underscore the fact that the stoning of Stephen was not an officially sanctioned act, nor was there any direct involvement of the Sanhedrin in any official capacity. There are no opposing or supporting witnesses, nor is any official decision declared, both of which we would expect from a legal meeting of the Sanhedrin. The charges against Stephen stem from his teachings about the law of Moses, which had been interpreted by his accusers as contrary to their own understanding; he was also accused of trying to alter the Law.

The text of Stephen's message to the group suggests that the words of Jesus were already being transmitted and passed on through the Christian community in the first two years after the resurrection. Stephen taught, "Jesus of Nazareth shall destroy this place [the temple]," a teaching that is reminiscent of what Jesus taught (consider the charge levied against Jesus during his arraignment before the Sanhedrin, and also a saying from the first year of his ministry; see Matthew 26:61; Mark 14:58; John 2:20). The wording of Acts 6:14 demonstrates that Stephen was actively passing on the teachings of Jesus and that the enemies of the faith were continuing to insist upon a literal interpretation of Jesus' saying about the destruction of the temple.

In the early church, the stoning of Stephen marked a turning point in the persecution of the church as well as a turning point in the missionary work of the church. The charges against Stephen brought to the forefront the question of whether or not one should be obedient to the law of Moses and whether living that law conflicted with being a faithful Christian.

Stephen's opponents viewed him not as an outsider believing in a different religion but as an insider who had corrupted their faith. Jews and pagans had learned to live in mutual toleration of one another, although Jews did not consider disrespect of pagan deities to be blasphemous. The speech of Stephen, however, was not viewed as the ramblings of an outsider with his own religious sentiments about a new pagan deity but as one who believed in Moses, the prophets, and God, but who nonetheless believed that there was another Deity in heaven—Jesus Christ. The shock of this must have been increased by Jesus' recent death and the likelihood that many in the audience knew of Jesus' public ministry. How could the man Jesus have joined the Father in heaven and even now be sitting at his right hand? The strength of Stephen's speech was that it was completely Jewish in outlook until the final moments, when he accused them of killing the prophets and not accepting God's emissaries (Acts 7:51–53). This was not the first such pointed rebuke by a prophet, and had Stephen ended at that point he may have returned home that fateful day. Another near contemporary of Stephen had declared the end of the temple in Jerusalem for many years, crying, "A voice from the east, a voice from the west, a voice from the four winds, a voice against Jerusalem and the holy house" (Josephus, *War,* 6.5.3). This prophet, named Jesus, was taken and given "a great number of severe stripes; yet did not he either say anything for himself" (Josephus, *War,* 6.5.3). Stephen, however, went on to testify that he had seen the heavens opened and that he could now see the exalted Lord, Jesus Christ, standing next to God in heaven (Acts 7:55–56). This final statement pushed his audience to the breaking point and they immediately covered their ears, a sign that they had heard blasphemy, and rushed toward Stephen.

Our first introduction to Paul in the New Testament comes at this juncture in the stoning of Stephen. Paul, Luke reports, was present at the stoning of Stephen as a witness of the events; he may have even been involved in some minor official capacity, as Luke implies when he states that those who served as official witnesses to the stoning of Stephen placed their outer cloaks at the feet of Paul, who seems to be acting as a recorder (Acts 7:58). Luke does not record enough detail to ascertain exactly what Paul's purpose was on that day, but the image left to us is one of a young man standing on the sidelines taking in the events and perhaps trying to understand their full meaning. Paul did not throw any stones, but the events of that day brought Paul out to see for himself what this new faith was about.

The ramifications of Stephen's speech were that Christians

could be believing Jews and that they viewed themselves as the inheritors of Jewish traditions. This speech and Stephen's eventual stoning opened the way for the gospel to spread rapidly through the Jewish Diaspora communities. Stephen himself was a Hellenistic Jew who had been called to administer to the Greek widows who had joined the church (Acts 6:1–5). Stephen was almost certainly not a native of Judea but had traveled to Jerusalem to participate in temple celebrations because of his association with the synagogue of the Libertines and had there been converted to Christianity. Clearly there must have been other men and women like Stephen, who had been prepared through Judaism to accept the gospel of Jesus Christ. The chronology of Acts supports this, as we learn that immediately after the death of Stephen, the apostles began to teach the gospel in Samaria, the first documented mission after the death of Jesus outside of Galilee and Judea. As part of these missionary efforts, the gospel was taught to the first foreigner—the Ethiopian eunuch.

Peter's vision of the sheet that unfolds, revealing to him that Gentiles were acceptable before God, is a part of this sequence of events. As the church began to expand and more Gentiles entered the church, the new leaders needed training on how to accept them into full fellowship. Paul must have realized the ramifications of what Stephen had taught and that they were no longer dealing with a localized heresy but that instead they could be facing a movement that could fracture Judaism from within.

PAUL ON THE ROAD TO DAMASCUS

Paul had foreseen the direction of the Christian church and its explosive potential for growth and therefore felt it to be an impending threat to his own beliefs. In response, Paul immediately stepped up his persecution against Christians (Acts 8:3).

Paul had also perceived how the church could grow outside of Jerusalem and sought to stem the tide of converts in Syria. He sought permission from the local Jewish leaders to travel to Damascus, a city one admirer called "a noteworthy city, having been, I might almost say, even the most famous of the cities in that part of the world in the time of the Persian empire" (Strabo, *Geography,* 16.2.20).

His attempts to arrest these so-called heretics must have relied upon local synagogue leaders who were willing to consent to the request to send their members back to Jerusalem for trial. Paul had no legal authority in the Roman Empire, but he must have felt that he could convince those local leaders of the urgency of stamping out this new movement and impeding its progress. If the local synagogue leaders did not cooperate with Paul's efforts to remand Christians back to Jerusalem for trial, then his efforts would prove futile; however, there is no evidence that such a decision had any legal authority. Perhaps Paul only hoped that Christians would travel to Jerusalem of their own accord. Historically, it is likely that Jews who were condemned as Christians faced local persecution or excommunication.

Paul's hope must have been that he could stem the tide and turn these converts away from their newfound faith through the threat of excommunication. Excommunication carried a serious stigma, and families would shun those who had been excommunicated. However, there was no clear indication that the threat of excommunication would be enough to change the minds of these Christians.

Perhaps Paul had sentiments similar to those expressed in a letter between a Jew and Christian writing several decades after Paul's time: "For Christians are no different from other people in terms of their country, language, or customs. Nowhere do they inhabit cities of their own, use a strange dialect, or live life out of the ordinary. They have not discovered this teaching of theirs through reflection or through the thought of meddlesome people, nor do they set forth any human doctrine, as do some. They inhabit both Greek and barbarian cities, according to the lot assigned to each. And they show forth the character of their own citizenship in a marvelous and admittedly paradoxical way by following local customs in what they wear and what they eat and in the rest of their lives" (*Epistle to Diognetus,* 5.1–4). The letter is dripping with scorn for Christians who, in the eyes of the author, are vagabonds. They have no country or traditions of their own, but feed like a parasite on other societies. The final line should not be taken as an endorsement, but rather a statement of surprise about how different the Christians were from the Jews.

Like others who were Pharisees or had Pharisaic leanings, Paul had to accept the fact that the Jews had a Sadduceean high priest; therefore, any official decision about the Christians would have to be made through compromise of these two religiously opposed sects. Paul may have been buoyed up in his efforts to impede the growth of Christianity because the Sadducees were staunch opponents of Jesus and according to the Gospel accounts were primarily responsible for the death of Jesus. He may have found an advocate in Joseph Caiaphas, who served as high priest from A.D. 18 to 36. That the family of Caiaphas were Sadducees seems to be implied by Josephus, who reports that Caiaphas's successor and brother-in-law "was also of the sect of the Sadducees" (*Antiquities,* 20.9.1).

Paul may also have been able to levy the charge of blasphemy against Christians, a charge that had worked so well against Jesus and Stephen. The charge of blasphemy against God, in the law of Moses, carried with it the punishment of stoning, but it had little if any force in Roman judicial proceedings. Paul could only hope that he was successful in his efforts to preserve the purity of his religion. On the fateful day that he traveled toward Damascus, he took with him colleagues who were probably likewise eager to buttress their ancestral faith. These traveling companions would later be able to verify that Paul had indeed had a remarkable experience and that his conversion to Christianity was genuine.

Paul traveled to Damascus unaware that his life was to change dramatically; he had made no preparations, and as far as we know he had had no impressions that he would become a brother to those he planned to persecute. Paul had been drawn into the arena of persecution as he saw the church making converts among not only Judean Jews but also among those who had ties throughout the Hellenistic world. As those converts traveled back to their homelands they could infect Jews everywhere with this new religion. Damascus was the city with the second largest concentration of church members. Paul probably desired to hinder the efforts of Christian missionaries who were working in that city. He believed he was carrying out God's will by strengthening the faith. But God had other plans on that day.

The account of the vision on the road to Damascus is told or referred to on at least five different occasions in the New Testament, thus testifying of its importance in the early church. Luke retold the story three separate times, and Paul himself referred to it directly on numerous occasions (Acts 9:3–9; 22:6–11; 26:13–18; Romans 10:2–4; 1 Corinthians 9:1; 15:8–10; 2 Corinthians 3–5; Galatians 1:16–17; Philippians 3:4–11). All three of the accounts in Acts mention that Paul traveled with companions, saw a bright light, and heard the voice of the Lord speaking to him from heaven. When Paul referred to the event personally, he spoke of it as a vision of the Lord in glory, who was revealed to him (Galatians 1:16) and who was seen by him (1 Corinthians 15:8). Paul was privileged to see what his companions only heard. Even though they were all present as witnesses to the same great event, Paul's personal account of that day is the only one to mention a direct vision of the resurrected Savior. The Lord spoke directly to Paul, and his traveling companions overheard their conversation. Unfortunately, we do not know whether Paul's companions ever joined the church, or whether they continued in their mission to persecute Christians.

The events on the road to Damascus stopped his journey and symbolically brought him to the judgment bar for a glimpse into his eternal destiny. Paul could have chosen to ascribe the vision to a moment of delusion or weakness or even to dismiss it as the workings of his own psyche, as many modern interpreters have done. Paul did not *have* to follow the voice, but his willingness to immediately do so demonstrates that his intentions to persecute the saints of Damascus was an act that he felt was acceptable to God. When he learned that his actions were contrary to the will of the Lord he immediately altered them to conform to what God had taught. Paul never looked back or questioned his new faith. He was essentially reborn through his vision of the resurrected Jesus Christ on the road to Damascus.

Interestingly, Paul never used the terms "foreordination" or "predestination" when he spoke of that experience. He would speak of foreordination to the Roman and Ephesian saints, but in describing his own experience he used the language of a prophetic call. To Paul, the road-to-Damascus experience did not follow from a foreordained calling but was the result of a prophetic call from God. Like the great prophets in Israel's past, Paul understood his vision as his own calling. Much like the wayward Alma in the Book of Mormon, the Lord had a work for Paul to do, and his path of persecution had led him far from it. On the day that the Lord appeared to him, He offered a sharp rebuke of Paul's actions and sent him to Ananias, a

Christian leader, for further instruction. Paul had to demonstrate his humility by following the directions of the Lord and by entrusting himself into the hands of those whom he had previously despised. Paul's submission to the church leaders in Damascus required a great restraint in his pride; he could never boast that he had been brought into the church with a full knowledge of its workings, but like all other members he had to become teachable.

The blinding light is an important element in the accounts of Paul's vision, one that is both literal and metaphorical. Paul, who up until that day had been absolutely convinced that he saw all things clearly, would learn from the Lord himself that he had been blinded. Paul had to learn to see again, to see things under the direction of church leaders. He had to learn how to follow instruction independent of his own training. Much has been said about Paul's education, origins, and upbringing, especially as they relate to his later work as an apostle. Paul would have viewed these endeavors as foolishness, since he himself taught that "what things were gain to me, those I counted loss for Christ" (Philippians 3:7). Paul learned to rely on the Lord, not his own Pharisaic scribal training. And as we will discuss later in greater detail, Paul's eyes were a source of great affliction to him, a thorn in the flesh to remind him that he had not always seen things as clearly as he believed.

Paul must have realized that in principle he had been judged on the day of his vision and had faced the judge of all mankind. His eternal progression had been redirected, and Paul must have felt the true weight of his actions for the first time. The shocking realization that his life needed redirection must have flooded over him with a wave of panic. Had the Lord smitten Paul that day, he would have borne the weight of his actions in eternity. The grace of the Lord, however, was invoked on Paul's behalf, and he was given another chance to do what had been in his heart all along: to truly serve the God of heaven. When the Lord spoke to him he said, "It is hard for thee to kick against the pricks" (Acts 9:5). We can almost see Paul traveling that dusty road in his open-toed Roman sandals in the heat of the day kicking against some unseen goad. The phrase "to kick against the pricks" has been obscured in the English of the King James Version. In a simple yet profound statement of divine logic, Jesus asked Paul, "Is it difficult to kick against a cactus?"

Chapter 3

THE POT BOILS OVER

"Though he once, according to his own word, persecuted the Church of God and wasted it, yet after embracing the faith, his labors were unceasing to spread the glorious news: and like a faithful soldier, when called to give his life in the cause which he had espoused, he laid it down, as he says, with an assurance of an eternal crown."
—Joseph Smith

With the voice of heaven ringing in his ears, Paul had the option—inspired by years of consistent obedience to the laws of Judaism—to reject or reinterpret the voice he had heard. Perhaps the story of Jonah was in the back of his mind, which teaches that those who reject the prophetic call end up engulfed by even greater problems. The appearance of the Lord to Paul on the road to Damascus reveals a careful balance between Paul's agency and the Lord making his desires clearly known. Interestingly the Lord did not tell Paul to become a Christian, but instead the Lord revealed to him His name and with sublime simplicity and eternal logic asked Paul whether kicking a cactus was worthwhile.

To those who have spent their lives in training to perform a single task or specialize in a certain field, the weight of Paul's decision is almost overwhelming. Paul had quickly risen to become a respected Pharisaic scribe but now found that he must become an entry-level Christian. Paul the Pharisaic scribe became Paul the new convert who needed fellowshipping and continued nourishment. The greatness of Paul lies not in what he saw on the Damascus road but in how he reacted to what he saw. No one can tell for certain which side of the pot the water will run down when it boils over, but the fact that the pot will soon boil over is always quite obvious. Paul, like all those of great faith, pointed himself toward the Lord and allowed Him to direct his movements, but it must be remembered that preconversion traits and habits are often prevalent in postconversion identity.

PAUL'S VISIT TO ANANIAS

As the Lord visited Paul on the road to Damascus he was also preparing a church leader, Ananias, to receive and teach a blinded persecutor. It must have been troubling for Ananias to be faced with blessing, and possibly healing, someone who had been so openly opposed to the church and who had been involved to some degree in the murder of a prominent church leader. Surprisingly, the early church continued to remember Ananias's open expression of concern to the Lord when he appeared in vision and told Ananias to accept Paul. Acts records that Ananias importuned the Lord, reminding him that this man had been a great hindrance to the growing church, saying, "Lord, I have heard by many of this man, how much evil he hath done to thy saints at Jerusalem" (Acts 9:13).

According to all written accounts of his experience on the road to Damascus, Paul was not told what his future role in the kingdom would be, although Acts records that the Lord taught this to Ananias (Acts 9:15). The book of Acts records that Paul was simply told to enter the city and someone would meet him there and give him further instructions (Acts 9:6; 22:10). Paul understood the vision on the road to Damascus as a call, but he was not told what he was called to do. That information would only come later through proper priesthood lines of authority. Only in the third retelling in Acts of what Paul experienced on the road to Damascus is there some intimation to Paul of his future. In this account the Lord said to Paul, "I have appeared unto thee for this purpose, to make thee a minister and a witness both of these things which thou hast seen, and of those things *in the which I will appear unto thee*" (Acts 26:16; emphasis added). The unanswered question was whether Paul would continue to rely on the Lord and become successful in his missionary endeavors.

Paul immediately began teaching among the Jews of the synagogue in Damascus. His teaching must have raised the ire of the Jews there not only because their former brother had left their ranks, but also because he had begun to teach the very falsehoods he had set out to destroy. The Jewish and Christian communities must have been closely associated in those days, because Paul's first attempt to teach the gospel took place in a Jewish synagogue. For him, the synagogue was the logical place to spread the good news. Acts does not mention the existence of house churches or houses that were used for churches in Antioch, or even separate places of worship for Christians in those days. Once Paul was converted he taught the gospel among other believers, and those believers were to be found either among the Jews in the synagogue or those who had associated themselves with the synagogue, such as the proselytes and god-fearers—believers who attended synagogue services but who were unwilling to be circumcised. This close association with the synagogue also explains Ananias's fear of accepting Paul, who had great influence among the members of the synagogue in Antioch.

Whether Paul was successful in Damascus during those initial weeks after his conversion is difficult to tell. In all likelihood his experiences there lasted only a few short weeks. Acts records that "Saul increased the more in strength, and confounded the Jews which dwelt at Damascus, proving that this is very Christ" (Acts 9:22). Once again the message focused on the divinity of Jesus Christ and likely away from the law of Moses—a dominant feature of the earliest message presented by Christian missionaries.

PAUL'S STAY IN ARABIA

Unknown to many is the fact that for nearly fourteen years after his conversion experience, Paul led a quiet life in the church learning its doctrines and following the inspired counsel of its leaders. Paul did not immediately become the apostle to the Gentiles, but instead soon fled to Arabia, an area then ruled by King Aretas IV. The "Arabs" were in reality the Nabataeans, who had in the past accepted Jews into their country but who were also preparing for war against Herod Antipas.

Reflecting back on this period of his ministry, Paul told the Galatian saints that after his vision he, "went . . . [not] up to Jerusalem to them which were apostles before me; but I went into Arabia, and returned again unto Damascus. Then after three years I went up to Jerusalem to see Peter, and abode with him fifteen days" (Galatians 1:17–18). Paul's account of his departure into Arabia reveals the difficulty of his conversion experience—not only was he now a Christian, but he had also lost his standing among his peers. In a few brief moments of time, Paul had gone from being a respected and esteemed Pharisee to a meek, lowly, and lay Christian. The difficulty arising from this change in status was compounded by the fact that at least some of his Christian brethren were skeptical of his conversion and intentions, therefore making Paul's continued presence in Damascus a potential stumbling-block for the saints.

Acts does not record, nor does Paul, the reasons why Paul left Damascus for Arabia shortly after his conversion. Perhaps his message was overshadowed by the fact that he had once persecuted those with whom he now sided. For Christians, Paul's recent conversion would need to stand the test of time; for Jews, it smacked of weakness, instability, and ignorance. The logical move at that point was away from Damascus and into a region where, uninhibited by Christian suspicion and Jewish disdain, he could spread the good news of the gospel he now embraced.

Paul seemingly went alone into Arabia. In all likelihood there were not many Christian missionaries in that area. An added concern for any who would dare venture with Paul into Arabia was the simple fact that he was a former persecutor. But why Arabia and not Tarsus, Antioch, or some other place familiar to Paul? The reasons for Paul's flight into Arabia are important to understanding the spiritual development of the future apostle.

THE DYNAMICS OF CONVERSION IN THE FIRST DECADES AFTER THE RESURRECTION

Today a physical requirement such as tithing can hinder acceptance of doctrinal beliefs. For many the principles of the gospel are easy enough to accept, but adding to those principles—as a means to confirm belief—can be overwhelming. Imagine if a requirement were not tithing but circumcision. It may appear strange that such a topic would be discussed in relation to early Christianity, but the earliest male members of the church were all Jewish and therefore circumcised. This rite was part of their religion and had almost certainly evolved into becoming part of their culture as well.

So what does this have to do with Paul? Several significant

obstacles hindered the success of the earliest Christian missionaries; one of them was the requirement that all males be circumcised as part of the conversion process. This requirement may have been the offspring of habit rather than a conscious decision by church leaders, but as the church expanded into Damascus, Antioch, Egypt, and beyond, it encountered societies among which circumcision was not practiced or accepted. The earliest missionary accounts do not record that circumcision was a prerequisite to becoming Christian or that it was actively taught, but the issue later became the major focus of a church-wide council in A.D. 49 in Jerusalem, where some, possibly misguided by tradition rather than doctrine, taught that all male members of the church had to be circumcised prior to being extended the hand of full fellowship in the church. They felt that circumcision was a matter of culture, practice, and religion and insisted on it for all new converts. The issue likely caused divisions within the first Christian communities as the first true gentile converts entered the church.

The first official church statement on the issue was given during the Jerusalem conference of A.D. 49, when the church leaders met to decide whether believing Gentiles had to obey the law of Moses and undergo circumcision. Acts records the issue, reporting that some were teaching that "except ye be circumcised after the manner of Moses, ye cannot be saved" (Acts 15:1). The discussion was heated and likely influenced the way the members presented the gospel to their friends and neighbors.

The church leaders presented a clear statement on the issue, likely reflecting their earlier unstated standing. At issue were both church doctrine and the perception of it by members, resulting in an uncomfortable crossroads where intentions, directed by tradition, could overshadow doctrine. Peter taught plainly, "Put no difference between us and them [the Gentiles]

. . . to put a yoke upon the neck of the disciples, which neither our fathers nor we were able to bear" (Acts 15:9–10). The decision, which resulted in part from Peter's inspired vision of the clean and unclean beasts, directed members of the church in gentile areas to forgo the requirement to be circumcised, while it appears the practice was continued in areas where the gospel was taught among the Jews.

In 49 A.D., then, the work of the church was set to proceed in earnest among the Gentiles—a direct result of the removal of the requirement that all males be circumcised prior to being accepted into full Christian fellowship. At the time of Paul's conversion, some sixteen years before the council's decision, the effects of this monumental decision were nonexistent. Paul converted in the day when the line between the two was not clearly demarcated. He may have perpetuated the misunderstanding himself, having recently entered the kingdom and having received little formal instruction.

The early Christian mission before the Jerusalem conference, therefore, would have been to those communities with a strong Jewish population, among the other descendants of Abraham who were not part of the house of Israel, who had similar traditions regarding circumcision. The Nabataeans were descendants of Abraham like the Jews, but they had not descended through the covenant line of Abraham, Isaac, and Jacob. According to popular tradition, the Nabataeans were descendants of Ishmael's oldest son, Nabaioth. Furthermore, the prophecy of Jeremiah 12:15—"And it shall come to pass, after that I have plucked them out I will return, and have compassion on them, and will bring them again, every man to his heritage, and every man to his land"—held out hope that the Lord would have compassion on the neighbors of Israel after they had departed from their tradition of worshipping idols. Isaiah 60:5–7 prophesies of a time when the Arab nations of Midian and

Ephah shall offer tribute in Jerusalem. For an early Christian missionary, these passages could have been interpreted as a doctrinal foundation for a mission to Arabia.

Paul, being well versed in scripture, may have had these very passages in mind when he set out for Arabia. A uniquely gentile mission would be difficult to support from the Old Testament, but Paul, knowing that in the future the Lord would bless Arabia, could have gone there feeling that the time of their redemption had arrived. Furthermore, he would be able to avoid the nearly insurmountable obstacles brought on by the topic of circumcision. In Arabia he would find other descendants of Abraham who had traditions similar to the Jews.

HEROD ANTIPAS AND ARETAS IV

Paul's experiences in Arabia were intimately related to the complex political environment of the region in the 30s. Paul, who certainly had no intention of engaging in politics in Arabia, was nonetheless caught up in the political difficulties that developed between King Aretas IV and Herod Antipas between A.D. 34 and A.D. 36. These difficulties were at their height when Paul was in the region. The length of time that Paul studied and taught in Arabia is unknown. He eventually returned to Damascus, where the hostility between Antipas and Aretas was still palpable. Paul was eventually threatened with death and forced to escape in secrecy. Fortunately, Paul did not seem to experience any long-lasting effects from what transpired in Arabia and Damascus thereafter. And certainly any theory that, as a Jew, Paul was in Arabia as part of a conspiracy against the Arabian government would have unraveled when the details surfaced concerning his mission to preach the gospel there.

A look at the events preceding Paul's mission to Arabia provides historical context for the suspicions such a visit created. At the death of Herod the Great (circa 4 B.C.), the lands surrounding the Dead Sea and the Sea of Galilee were divided among three of Herod's sons: Archelaus, Herod Antipas, and Herod Philip. Herod Antipas, popularly referred to as Herod in the New Testament (Matthew 2), received the areas of Galilee and Perea—the area to the east of the Jordan River between the Sea of Galilee and the Dead Sea.

In a move to create new political alliances, Herod Antipas married an Arabian princess, one of the daughters of Aretas IV, probably Shayudat. Aretas IV, a Nabataean king, ruled Arabia from roughly 9 B.C. to A.D. 40. The marriage between one of the leading scions of the Herodian dynasty and one of Aretas's daughters promised to pave the way for political and economic partnerships between the two nations; it also promised to offer peace on the eastern frontier of the Roman empire, something that was valuable to the Herodian family and of particular interest to the Roman imperial government.

Antipas, while visiting Rome on business in the early 30s, became infatuated with his brother Philip's wife, and the two of them conspired upon their return from Rome to divorce their spouses and marry. This sultry relationship caught the attention of the great Jewish historian Josephus, who chronicled the event; it also eventually drew the condemnation of John the Baptist, who denounced the marriage as unlawful according to Mosaic law. Herod's love of Herodias proved to be the fruit of blind passion and lust, and shortly after his return to Galilee in about A.D. 30 he divorced his Arabian princess. King Aretas was enraged by the divorce and sought for the remainder of his life to take revenge on Antipas for shaming his daughter. Aretas was eventually successful in vanquishing Antipas, convincingly defeating his army in A.D. 36 (*Antiquities*, 18.5.1–2).

One first-century report remembers the hatred that existed between Herod and Aretas after the divorce: "Aretas also, the king of Arabia Petrea out of his hatred to Herod, and in order to purchase the favor of the Romans, sent him no small assistance, besides their footmen and horsemen: and when he had now collected all his forces together, he committed part of them to his sons, and to a friend of his, and sent them upon an expedition into Galilee, which lies in the neighborhood of Ptolemais; who made an attack upon the enemy, and put them to flight, and took Sepphoris [north of Nazareth], and made its inhabitants slaves, and burnt the city" (*Antiquities*, 17.10.9).

Paul's visit to Arabia and subsequent return to Damascus coincided with a period of increasing hostility toward Jews in the Nabataen government. When Herod Philip died in A.D. 34, Aretas attempted to seize Philip's former territories, which were south and immediately east of Damascus. This, of course, angered Antipas, who also sought leadership of these lands.

Imagine the reaction when Paul—a Jew—entered this volatile political environment, where the reigning king was skeptical of Jews in general and was specifically angry with Antipas, who had offended both his family name and his daughter. It is quite possible that Paul's rejection in Arabia may have had nothing to do with the nature of his message but with what might have been perceived as a political threat.

The length of Paul's stay in Arabia is unknown; but it could not have lasted much longer than two years. He mentions his time in Arabia on two separate occasions, but tells us nothing of his success or failure (2 Corinthians 11:32; Galatians 1:17). For the first part of his ministry there, Paul appears to have had open and free access to all regions of the country, and he leaves us no hint that he was unwelcome there or that he felt threatened. Arabia had a large enough Jewish population that he would have found at least some sanctuary among his fellow countrymen, particularly, we would expect, among Christian converts. (Because he was so far from his homeland, he was likely among people who had not received news of his previous role as a persecutor of Christians.)

From the perspective of an outsider, Paul's activities in Arabia, and later Damascus, may have been suspicious. Paul stayed in close contact with Jews and with local synagogues and taught them new doctrines originating from a Jewish Messiah. At the same time, the Nabataeans had been offended by Antipas, a Jew, and were preparing for war. Because of the tension between Aretas and Antipas, Paul's intentions in Arabia may have been interpreted politically rather than spiritually, and any success Paul had may have caught the attention of local authorities who were eager to maintain peace with Aretas and distance themselves from the ongoing political intrigues.

As Paul later told the story, the conspiracy to apprehend him was more widespread than simply a local governor trying to expel him—and the breadth of that conspiracy presents another interesting possibility for his rejection in Arabia. Perhaps Paul fled Arabia for Damascus after an uprising of Jews against him, which could have included a threat against his life. This could have been much like the event that took place in Corinth nearly two decades later and resulted in Paul being charged with insurrection: some who heard his new doctrines regarding the Jewish Messiah started a revolt against Paul (Acts 18:12–17). Depending on how Paul intended "three years" to be counted, Paul could have remained in Damascus for as little as two (parts of years one and three and all of year two) to nearly three complete years. Acts condenses the story into a short, seven-verse narrative, while Paul explains that it was a three-year period (Acts 9:19–26; Galatians 1:17).

After Paul's return to Damascus, King Aretas tried to arrest him, even though he did not directly govern the city. As Paul recorded, "The governor under Aretas the king kept the city of the Damascenes with a garrison, desirous to apprehend me: and through a window in a basket was I let down by the wall, and escaped his hands" (2 Corinthians 11:32–33).

Not all Christians in Damascus were under the same threat as Paul, and the Christians appear to be the ones who smuggled him out of the city. Aretas was not anti-Christian but anti-Paul, suggesting a direct correlation between Paul's missionary activity and Aretas's attempt to arrest him. In fact, Paul's statements say that the king was trying to "apprehend me" (2 Corinthians 11:32), but he makes no mention that others were sought for arrest.

Acts adds another dimension to the story by relating that "after that many days were fulfilled, the Jews took counsel to kill him: But their laying await was known of Saul. And they watched the gates day and night to kill him" (Acts 9:23–24). While Paul's account of the event focused on Aretas as the instigator of the attempt to arrest Paul, Luke focused on the Jewish agents in the city of Damascus, without mentioning Aretas.

What caused such a stir among Aretas and a handful of Jews is revealed only through innuendo and implication. Paul's teaching in Arabia may have been too persuasive, causing a commotion in the Jewish community, who reported Paul's activities to Aretas. The king, who had been misinformed, sought to capture Paul as a political prisoner. The charge would almost certainly have been insurrection. After Paul had returned to Damascus, he found out about Aretas's further attempt to take him by stealth.

The information that Paul was about to be arrested may have come from Jews or Jewish Christians in Damascus who supported Paul and believed in his message. Luke is almost certainly correct when he associates the opposition in Damascus after Paul's return from Arabia as Jewish, but it would have been Jews who were complicit in some way with Aretas and his local agents. This pattern of a divided audience became a familiar theme throughout the apostle's ministry. Paul the persecutor had now become Paul the persecuted. He had gained first-hand experience of being threatened, hiding, trusting his safety to others, and relying on whispers and rumors of what was about to come to pass.

Paul's travels in Arabia taught him to teach the gospel in power and provided him an opportunity to work through the scriptures and learn how Jesus fulfilled the prophecies of the Messiah, but it did not teach him about the Christian church. He could learn about the kingdom only from those who had already been converted. In the early 30s, Christianity had not spread much beyond Jerusalem and Galilee, and certainly only a very few had traveled to Arabia. Paul did not travel to Arabia to find Christians but to find himself, which he did in preaching the gospel.

Paul's first years after his conversion were an exercise in learning humility. The fiery Pharisaic scribe became an active missionary, embarking on a mission to a land that had not previously received the gospel of Jesus Christ. Neither Luke nor Paul himself relate that he sought instruction on how or where to teach the gospel, but instead he appears to have set out according to his own desires or perhaps as directed by an unrecorded revelation. In this aspect of his early mission, he may have relied too heavily on his own judgment, being misled by his own zeal to demonstrate his sincerity to those who questioned his genuineness and being led on by his own yearnings to obtain forgiveness for his actions against Christians.

The church was certainly small enough to permit access to its leadership by such a well-known convert. And Paul was now a huge asset. But he did not immediately seek guidance beyond what he had been given in Damascus.

Several possible answers exist that would satisfactorily

explain Paul's decision not to return directly to Jerusalem after his conversion experience on the road to Damascus. The solution lies in a mixture and combination of all of them. First, Paul did not travel to Jerusalem immediately to meet with the apostles because he did not view them as a separate religion from Judaism, and therefore he was not aware of the need to seek counsel separate from the training he had already received. Second, an overwhelming sense of guilt and repentance seem to have directed his initial movements into Arabia, Damascus, and beyond. Third, Paul would have been under the suspicion of the Jerusalem authorities who had sent him to Damascus, and therefore a return to Jerusalem may have cost him his life, or even worse, that of his family.

PAUL'S FIRST VISIT TO JERUSALEM

When Paul finally visited Jerusalem more than three years after his conversion, he sought to meet the leaders of the Christian church (Galatians 1:18). Peter had been a resident of Capernaum in Galilee during Jesus' mortal ministry, but when Paul sought him out he found him in Jerusalem. Perhaps in Jesus' call to the disciples they were required to permanently leave all that they had, including their employment and homes in Galilee. Paul stayed with Peter for fifteen days, no doubt asking questions and learning about the life of Jesus, for which there was yet no written account. Paul must have learned a great deal about Jesus from Peter because his later letters are ornamented with allusions to and reminiscences of Jesus' life.

A courtesy call need not extend longer than a day or two, but a visit of fifteen days suggests that Paul was doing more than making his conversion known. Arabia had taught him that he could not endeavor to teach the gospel on his own and that he needed further instruction before embarking on another mission. Likely during that same visit Peter was able to receive a full account of Paul's conversion.

A bond of friendship must have developed between the two, and Peter remained his priesthood leader throughout his life, because Paul later returned to Jerusalem seeking Peter when he ran into troubles at the end of his first missionary journey. Paul relied on Peter for instruction, and Peter would later accept correction from Paul. The two of them remained friends throughout their lives.

Paul also met with James, the brother of Jesus, who had by this time converted to Christianity (Galatians 1:19). James had not been a follower of Jesus during Christ's mortal ministry, but converted sometime shortly after Jesus' death. Paul lists James as one of the people who was privileged to see the glorified and resurrected Savior, and by the early 30s Paul calls him an apostle (1 Corinthians 15:7; Galatians 1:19). The exact role of James in the leadership of the church is unclear in this early period, but Paul calling him an apostle is important because it offers a second witness to the earliness of James's conversion.

The prerequisites of an apostle given in Acts 1 may explain why Paul referred to James as such—perhaps he met the requirements as a personal witness of the resurrected Savior even though he may not have been ordained one of the Twelve. When the apostles were choosing a replacement for Judas, Peter stipulated that they should choose from the group of men "which have companied with us all the time that the Lord Jesus went in and out among us, beginning from the baptism of John, unto that same day that he was taken up from us"—such were the requirements of one who could be "ordained to be a witness with us of his resurrection" (Acts 1:21–22). To be an apostle, then, one had to have been with Jesus from the time of John's baptism, as well as having been a witness to the Resurrection. James filled this definition even though he was not a believer in

Jesus early on. Paul's reference to James as an apostle most likely relies on this definition, for he also relates that James saw the resurrected Lord separately from "all the apostles," who are also listed as distinct from the Twelve Apostles (1 Corinthians 15:5, 7).

THE STATUS OF THE CHURCH IN JERUSALEM ABOUT A.D. 35

Paul's visit to Jerusalem about A.D. 35 raises a number of important questions regarding the status of the church in the holy city. As mentioned previously, Paul had not felt that a visit to the apostles or other church leaders in Jerusalem was necessary before embarking on his mission into Arabia, perhaps because he had received sufficient direction in Damascus. After being driven from Damascus through threats on his life—and with little evidence of success in his earlier travels to Arabia—Paul finally turned to Jerusalem for guidance. Paul's maturity in the gospel was certainly increasing, and he likely felt a growing need to find out more about Jesus from those who knew him personally, but the fact that he met with only Peter and James in Jerusalem is somewhat startling.

Acts records that several of the apostles had remained in the city of Jerusalem for some time after the death of Jesus; however, the record indicates only that Paul met with Peter and James (the Lord's brother). The author of Acts, who fails to mention this early visit of Paul to Jerusalem, gives the impression that many of the apostles still lived in and around Jerusalem about A.D. 35 when Paul visited. A veritable ocean of possibilities present themselves as to why Paul may not have met with James the son of Zebedee, or John, or any of the leading apostles from the period of Jesus' mortal ministry.

The answer is not likely to be found in a fractured church or the flight of the apostles, but in the type of information that

Paul came seeking. Paul had been baptized, had received the Holy Ghost, and presumably had been ordained to the priesthood—although this is not recorded in any source—but he had yet to come in contact with anyone who knew Jesus personally. The names of the Christians Paul had met at that point are not recorded in the Gospels, suggesting that like Paul they were later converts. Paul chose to seek out Jesus' leading apostle and closest associate—although any of Jesus' apostles could have provided the same information—as well as the younger brother of Jesus who, like Paul, did not believe in Jesus initially.

The information that Paul sought does not appear to have been about church doctrine or organization only, but rather something that very few individuals could provide—a detailed account of Jesus' life. The fact that Paul would seek such information and not further guidance—and the fact that he made no special plea for position within the church—bears testimony of his humble willingness to accept whatever direction he received.

PAUL'S RETURN TO TARSUS?

From his later epistle to Philemon—written nearly thirty years after his first visit to Jerusalem, where Paul calls himself "aged" (Philemon 1:9)—it appears that Paul was nearing his early sixties. If this information is correct, then Paul was most likely in his thirties when he visited Jerusalem to meet with Peter, and about thirty at the date of his conversion. As a fiery young convert to the church, who had recently returned from a mission where King Aretas sought to take his life and where he also met with very little or no success, Paul was now faced with the decision of what to do next. He had no specific church calling that would take him back into the missionary field, he had no special employment that would direct his relocation, and his life was in danger in Damascus and possibly in Jerusalem also, where his old contacts had certainly heard about his conversion to Christianity.

The next time that Paul is mentioned in Acts, he is in Antioch (Acts 11:25–26), about 150 miles from his hometown in Tarsus. Antioch, at the time of Paul, was a thriving metropolis with a considerable Jewish population. Josephus notes that "Antioch . . . is the metropolis of Syria, and, without dispute, deserves the place of the third city in the habitable earth that was under the Roman empire, both in magnitude and other marks of prosperity" (*War,* 3.2.4).

This period of Paul's life is the most overlooked in modern studies, as well as being the most overlooked by Acts and the apostle himself. For some reason, neither felt that this period of Paul's early career was important for understanding the later developments in Paul's life—or perhaps Luke was largely unaware of this period in his life. Paul, with his usual reticence to speak about his personal life, kept silent about the period. Paul relates that his immediate direction after his first visit to Jerusalem was into the regions of "Syria and Cilicia," which would include Damascus, Antioch, and Tarsus (Galatians 1:21). Luke notes that "the disciples were called Christians first in Antioch," probably a recognition of the fact that Jews and Christians were more distinctly recognizable as separate groups there (Acts 11:26). In Judea and Galilee, Christians were initially viewed as Jewish heretics, and calling them Christians would designate them as a separate sect, something Jews were unwilling to do in the 30s and 40s. In Antioch, however, Gentiles recognized early on that Christians and Jews were separate sects; therefore, they were the first to develop a distinct name for them.

As Paul left Jerusalem after interviewing Peter and James, the brother of Jesus, he found himself going home, without pomp and circumstance, without any significant calling, and without any particular recognition by the Jerusalem authorities. Perhaps he went home to teach the gospel to his family. Paul spent fourteen years between his first visit to Jerusalem and his second visit—when the historical sources begin again to report his life in considerable detail.

From the scantiness of the historical record of this fourteen-year period, we can assume that he located the nearest branch of the Church and began participating in their services. Acts identifies a congregation in Antioch, but there may also have been one in Tarsus. No mention is made of Paul's family in Antioch during the period; the only secure biographical reference to his family and place of origins places them in Tarsus. Only a passing reference to a nephew and sister at the end of his life remains (Acts 23:16). If he indeed returned to Tarsus hoping to convert his family, then no report of it was made, and unfortunately no report is made of any stunning successes or failures. Like many, his family may have viewed his new religious interest with indifference, particularly given the fact that he had previously embraced Judaism with such fire and zeal.

BETWEEN JERUSALEM AND THE FIRST MISSION

Because we have scant information about the beginnings of the first mission of Paul and Barnabas, it is impossible to know its duration. However, the surviving picture of the early years before the return to Jerusalem is one of solitude, quiet learning, dedicated service, and growth. We can almost sense the passion and boundless drive of the apostle Paul as he labored in the missionary frontiers of the regions around Antioch in Syria and Cilicia. His initial efforts to spread the gospel had begun with a fervor that was previously unmatched in the annals of Christian history; he was the first missionary to attract any considerable mention outside the confines of Judea and Palestine. Certainly some of the fascination with Paul was a direct result of his having been a former persecutor of the new Messianic faith, but in addition he attracted the gaze of the official church history because of his uncompromising stance and undying fervor to take the message of the Lord Jesus Christ to all nations. The apostles, at least for the first few years of the church's existence, were busying themselves with the organization of the church and seeing to the daily needs of its members, while at the same time holding ardently to the faith in spite of Jewish aggression.

For men with such unbridled zeal for the gospel, nothing could be more stifling than to sit idly by and learn of the continued opposition that the disciples were facing in and around Jerusalem. The earliest apostles had all grown up in the regions around Judea and Galilee, and they must have felt the need to have some initial success in the Jewish heartland before they took the gospel to the non-Israelite nations. That initial success in Jerusalem did come quickly, but with it came the need to administer to the needs of the new converts as well as to establish the foundation for living the law of consecration (Acts 2:41; 5:1–11). Paul, on the other hand, lived on the frontier of the Christian mission and must have experienced firsthand the paucity of members, especially in the late 30s and early 40s. Moreover, he had grown up in the Diaspora, or among other scattered Israelites, and knew of the strength and vitality of Judaism outside the Jewish homeland.

CONCLUSION

The true and enduring strength of the apostle Paul is manifest in his humble and patient attitude in the long years between his conversion near Damascus and his first missionary journey with Barnabas. He had exploded onto the scene of Christianity with a burst of energy that led him into uncharted territories and deep into a plot that threatened his life. As far as we can tell the mission was not very successful, and Paul returned to Damascus, eventually traveling to Jerusalem to gather further information and guidance. But that mission's purpose went beyond finding converts: the mission to the Nabataeans or eastern Arab peoples under Aretas's domain was to teach Paul the fundamentals of the gospel. That gospel training continued in the post-Jerusalem period in a small branch, through the inspired leaders of those branches as well as the fine-tuned direction of the Holy Ghost. Paul certainly had the drive to begin a new missionary effort, but he likely lacked the basic training that would make him a successful missionary.

The decade or so he spent in and around Antioch bridled Paul in a way, bringing his passions and fire into harmony with the Brethren, teaching him that all were alike in Christ. Local leaders, as they do in so many instances today, provided valuable and skilled training to one of the greatest missionaries the church has ever had. The greatness of Paul's character was manifest in his humble submission to training, through which he also learned the valuable life lesson that revelation comes through church leaders. Without an understanding of these eternal truths, Paul would have faltered in his later missionary efforts. Instead, he learned by experience a truth he repeatedly taught: that usurpers and interlopers could be detected because they did not follow the divinely ordained order of God. Paul must have certainly been an outspoken participant in those early days of training, as his later epistles would lead us to believe, but in those quiet moments, behind the official registers of Christian history, Paul learned what it meant to be a Christian.

Chapter 4

PAUL'S MISSION WITH BARNABAS

"He is about five feet high; very dark hair; dark complexion; dark skin; large Roman nose; sharp face; small black eyes, penetrating as eternity; round shoulders; a whining voice, except when elevated, and then it almost resembled the roaring of a lion. He was a good orator, active and diligent, always employing himself in doing good to his fellow man."
—Joseph Smith

Assuming that Paul was indeed in his early thirties when he converted to the gospel of Jesus Christ, then Paul would have been nearly fifty years old at the time of his return to Jerusalem when he reported the success and difficulties of his first official mission to Cyprus—the hometown of Barnabas—and central Asia.

Very few clues remain concerning details of the period between Paul's return trip to Antioch and Cilicia after his visit with Peter and James in Jerusalem and his subsequent mission to Cyprus and the interior of central Asia. From Galatians comes the detail that fourteen years passed between Paul's first visit with Peter in Jerusalem and his return there with Barnabas and Titus at the end of his mission to Cyprus and Asia

(Galatians 2:1). Almost nothing is known of the years prior to Barnabas going to find Paul, but if their mission to Cyprus lasted about three to four years, then Paul's time alone in the regions where his family lived lasted about ten years.

Late in Paul's life, during his final arrest in Jerusalem, a plot to take his life was foiled by the help of "Paul's sister's son" who went and told Paul that certain Jews had taken an oath not to eat until they had taken the apostle's life (Acts 23:12–16). This lone biographical reference is perhaps the only piece of evidence suggesting that Paul's early missionary work in his hometown and the surrounding regions met with any success. Paul's nephew was obviously willing to help him out in a time of great need, and clearly took a position that was hostile to the Jewish leadership of Jerusalem, a decision that could translate into trouble for his family later. Such evidence is hardly substantial enough to make any firm conclusions about Paul's family's conversion or to imply that his mission in Tarsus was successful, but it does show that Paul continued to have a positive relationship with at least a portion of his family.

Paul, during his ten-year stay in Tarsus and the neighboring regions, continued to remain faithful and did not attract the attention of the leaders of the church in Jerusalem. Luke is completely silent on Paul's whereabouts and doings during this period. One first-century geographer makes Paul's return and stay in Tarsus appear out of the ordinary when he reports, "But it [Tarsus] is so different from other cities that there the men who are fond of learning are all natives, and foreigners are not inclined to sojourn there; neither do these natives stay there, but they [the natives] complete their education abroad; and when they have completed it they are pleased to live abroad, and but few go back home. . . . In general it not only has a flourishing population but also is most powerful, thus keeping up the reputation of the mother-city" (Strabo, *Geography*, 14.5.13).

A general impression exists that Paul, immediately after his conversion on the road to Damascus, became a great missionary to the gentile cities of the Mediterranean. This impression, unfortunately, does not correlate well with the historical reports from the time period. Unlike Alma the younger, who almost immediately became the leader of the churches in Zarahemla (Alma 1:2; 4:18), Paul spent a considerable amount of time piecing together his life, reflecting on his past, and almost certainly preaching the gospel among the people he knew. A long-time stay in the idyllic surroundings of Tarsus would have given Paul ample time to rethink his Pharisaic training and to ponder the words of Jesus that he had received from Peter and James in Jerusalem. Tarsus could also provide a generous living: "And the nature of the region is wonderful, for among the summits of the Taurus [Mountains] there is a country which can support tens of thousands of inhabitants and is so very fertile that it is planted with the olive in many places, and with fine vineyards, and produces abundant pasture for cattle of all kinds; and above this country, all round it, lie forests of various kinds of timber. . . . It is remarkably productive of sheep; but the wool is coarse, and yet some persons have acquired very great wealth from this alone" (Strabo, *Geography,* 12.7.3; 12.6.1). Tarsus thus had two important features to offer Paul, besides being the residence of his family; it supported countless people to whom Paul could preach the gospel, and it provided employment opportunities. What can be seen in Paul's life during this period is a true development of character. The person who emerged from Tarsus the second time was equally zealous to teach the gospel, but that zeal was tempered by reason and love, something that was lacking when Paul began to persecute Christians. Paul the missionary was also extremely well versed in the Old Testament prophecies of Jesus Christ and how the law of Moses brought the children of Israel to Christ. Perhaps the foremost lesson that

Paul learned while he sojourned in Tarsus is that the most significant and enduring development of character takes place behind closed doors, away from the spotlight, in humble solitude and submission to the Lord's will. Paul's zeal was never in question, but his humble submission and endurance were.

BARNABAS SEARCHES OUT PAUL

Developments in Jerusalem made it increasingly clear that the gospel would spread beyond the regions of Judea and Galilee. In the area of Judea, the Lord was beginning to prepare the hearts of Gentiles to hear the gospel. For example, Cornelius, a gentile centurion of Caesarea, had a vision in which he saw a messenger, Simon Peter, who would teach him the gospel (Acts 10:3–6). Cornelius is called "a centurion of the band called the Italian band," which indicates that he served in the *Cohors Italica,* the Roman legion stationed in Syria (Acts 10:1). Cornelius was probably one of six centurions in the cohort, each of whom commanded one hundred men; he would also have been a man of influence and rank in the region, with many friends. Luke reports that Cornelius was living in Caesarea, an indication that he had either retired from the military or was on special assignment there, for it is unlikely that the Roman cohort would have been stationed in the region while Agrippa I ruled (A.D. 41–44).

Cornelius, a Roman citizen and respected military leader, became a lynchpin for the spread of the gospel into other predominantly gentile communities. If he converted to the gospel and subsequently taught it to a few of his friends, then the gospel message would have a door through which it could begin to spread more quickly beyond Judea and Galilee.

While Cornelius was being prepared to receive the gospel, Peter was being prepared to teach the gospel to a pure Gentile. Peter, who expressed some concerns over taking the gospel to

Gentiles, understood the full impact of the vision of clean and unclean beasts he had received and therefore went to Caesarea to teach Cornelius the gospel. When Peter arrived he reminded Cornelius, "Ye know how that it is an unlawful thing for a man that is a Jew to keep company, or come unto one of another nation; but God hath shewed me that I should not call any man common or unclean" (Acts 10:28). Peter appears to have still felt some hesitancy to enter the house of a Gentile, and refers to himself as "a Jew." Cornelius, on the other hand, had assembled "many" of his friends and family so that they could hear the gospel (Acts 10:27).

The impression created by Acts is that Cornelius was one of the first, if not the first, Gentile to convert to the gospel after the death of Jesus. Prior to that time the gospel had spread among Jews. Even Cornelius seems to have been a follower of Judaism to some extent prior to his conversion. Acts calls him "a devout man, and one that feared God with all his house" (Acts 10:2). But Peter's uneasiness and concern give the impression that entering the home of a Gentile was new to him. The conversion of Cornelius and his friends set into motion a series of events that would significantly alter the course of the church.

Immediately after Cornelius's conversion, word traveled back to Jerusalem that "the Gentiles had also received the word of God" (Acts 11:1). When Peter returned to Jerusalem, "they that were of the circumcision contended with him" (Acts 11:2). The issue of circumcision had not yet been fully resolved in the church; therefore, some assumed that all converts had to follow the ancestral customs and laws of the Jews. This faction within the church complained specifically about Peter's interaction with Cornelius and the fact that he had entered into their home, "and didst eat with them" (Acts 11:3). Luke clarifies that the rift did not end in a split but instead, "When they heard these things [Peter's vision], they held their peace, and glorified God, saying, Then hath God also to the Gentiles granted repentance unto life" (Acts 11:18). Luke's wording suggests that this was a novel idea.

The whole issue of whether Gentiles could be accepted into full fellowship as Christians may seem rather odd from a modern perspective, but the reality of the Jerusalem branch(es) was that they continued to struggle over which members were still required to live all aspects of the law of Moses (Acts 15).

After describing the meeting in Jerusalem, Luke introduces Barnabas, a native of Cyprus and a missionary who had been preaching the gospel outside of Jerusalem. These missionaries were careful to take the gospel to "the Jews only" (Acts 11:19). One of these early missionaries, Barnabas, must have found that the work was proceeding slowly and as a result began teaching the gospel to Greeks (Acts 11:20). This shift resulted in the conversion of many Gentiles, "and a great number believed, and turned unto the Lord" (Acts 11:21). The early part of Acts begins with accounts of explosive growth in Judea, but then gives the impression that there was a lull in conversions and that the missionary work had begun to stagnate. Cornelius, in Luke's account, opened a new door for the gospel, the door to the gentile mission.

These three streams—Peter's vision of the gentile mission, Cornelius's acceptance of the gospel, and Barnabas's teaching the gospel to Greeks—all converged into a single mighty river. They appear to have happened at the same time in three different locales. Peter, realizing the potential for a true gentile mission, sent Barnabas to Antioch to preach the gospel. Barnabas, who had no doubt heard about Paul, stopped at Tarsus on his way and sought out Paul (Acts 11:25). Luke's awkward wording hints that Paul was not found easily, but that Barnabas literally had to search for him. Perhaps, like other missionaries of that early period, Paul had eventually met some stiff resistance and had gone into hiding. Or, it may simply have been that in an age before phone books and easily available city maps, it was hard to find people in ancient cities. Luke records that Paul, following the direction of the Spirit, willingly left his hometown behind and traveled with Barnabas to Antioch, a subtle hint that he may have been ready to leave Tarsus.

Barnabas then took Paul to Antioch, where both of them served in the branch "a whole year" (Acts 11:26). Luke records that "the disciples were called Christians first in Antioch" (Acts 11:26). This statement takes on additional meaning when we realize that this is the first time, as Barnabas and now Paul began to teach the gospel to Gentiles, that anyone needed a new term to distinguish between Jews and the followers of Christ. Prior to this time, Christianity was called the "way," which in the eyes of their contemporaries meant that followers of Christ were Jews who believed that Jesus was the Messiah, who taught another "way" to be Jewish (Acts 9:2). Now, only after the mission to the Gentiles became successful, was there a need for a term to distinguish those who converted to Christ but who had never been Jews.

Barnabas seems to have been the person called to head up that mission. Peter, however, did not explicitly give Barnabas instructions on who to call and how to proceed but instead left many of those decisions in the hands of Barnabas (Acts 13:1–2).

Barnabas, realizing the potential of Paul, went to Tarsus personally to find him and call him to this new missionary undertaking. In this setting, under the direction and guiding hand of the Spirit, Paul showed that his time spent in the forge of the Lord had brought forth a beautifully wrought tool whose malleability had rendered him both adaptable and resilient.

THE FAMINE IN THE DAYS OF CLAUDIUS

Shortly after Barnabas and Paul departed for Cyprus, a severe famine began to affect Italy, Greece, Judea, and elsewhere. The famine was a direct result of drought, and the poorer areas of the Roman Empire felt the effects most profoundly. According to Josephus, "Now her coming [Queen Helena of Adiabene] was of very great advantage to the people of Jerusalem; for whereas a famine did oppress them at that time, and many people died for want of what was necessary to procure food withal, queen Helena sent some of her servants to Alexandria with money to buy a great quantity of corn, and others of them to Cyprus, to bring a cargo of dried figs; and as soon as they were come back, and brought those provisions, which was done very quickly, she distributed food to those that were in want of it, and left a most excellent memorial behind her of this benefaction, which she bestowed on our whole nation" (*Antiquities*, 20.2.5). The famine in Jerusalem at the time of the emperor Claudius (A.D. 41–54) was so severe, in fact, that Josephus mentioned it on three separate occasions.

The Judean famine became the first real test of the fledgling church network in the Mediterranean, as "the disciples" were asked to send to Jerusalem whatever commodities they could spare at the time (Acts 11:29). Acts records that they were to send, "every man according to his ability" to give "relief unto the brethren which dwelt in Judaea" (Acts 11:29). Some have mistakenly taken this to mean that each man could collect what he could and do with it as he saw fit. Such a policy would certainly lead to corruption and appears unlikely, given the situation. Luke relates that each man was to gather whatever he could, according to his ability to do so. He then records how Barnabas and Paul were able to make a collection for the saints affected by the famine. Furthermore, Luke does not mention any other individuals by name, hinting that Barnabas and Paul were the foremost disciples in gathering the collection because of their influence, efforts, and network of contacts. This is the first indication in Acts that Paul was different from his peers within the church. His tireless efforts to help relieve the suffering of the saints in Judea may have had special meaning to him as he considered how he had previously persecuted the church in Judea.

At this point in the narrative, Luke interrupts the story of Barnabas and Paul to relate the death of the apostle James, who died in A.D. 44 under the hands of Herod Antipas. The reasons for interrupting the narrative are not entirely clear, because the story of James's death could easily have been told after the account of the famine and the relief efforts had been completed. Bracketing both ends of the story of James's martyrdom is the gathering of food for the suffering saints, which is collected and then delivered to Jerusalem by Barnabas and Paul (Acts 11:30; 12:25).

Paul's visit to Jerusalem to bring aid may have contributed in some way to the arrest and condemnation of James the son of Zebedee and the subsequent flight of Peter to Caesarea. Peter, who had lived continually in Jerusalem since shortly after the resurrection of Christ, was arrested shortly after the death of James but was delivered by an angel. Upon his escape, he spent the night at the home of the mother of John Mark, who was a nephew to the famous missionary Barnabas and who later wrote the Gospel of Mark, and then later fled to Caesarea (Acts 12:2–4, 7–10, 12, 18–19). Paul's presence in Jerusalem may have embittered the mobs who, finding that their old nemesis was back in town, lashed out at those who harbored or assisted him.

PAUL AND BARNABAS DEPART

Paul continued to serve in Antioch, where he is grouped with those who were called, "prophets and teachers" (Acts

13:1). From among this group of five—Barnabas, Simeon Niger, Lucius of Cyrene, Manaen, and Paul—the Lord chose two to set out on the first truly gentile mission in the church. Luke clearly implies that Barnabas was chosen to lead the mission by placing his name first whenever he makes any reference to Barnabas and Paul. Their destination is not explicitly mentioned in the account of their call, but Barnabas was a Levite from Cyprus; and therefore, this mission, like Paul's return to Tarsus, was to Barnabas's hometown (Acts 4:36; 13:4).

After traveling overland to the nearby seaport of Seleucia, Paul and Barnabas set sail for Cyprus. The two disciples would have traveled the short distance of sixteen miles between Antioch and Seleucia on foot, reaching the breathtaking shoreline of the Mediterranean in a day or two. From a distance they could see the acropolis of Seleucia on Mount Pierius.

The city of Seleucia was built into a hillside with the residential neighborhood built into it in a terraced fashion. While in Seleucia, Barnabas and Paul would have had to wait until a packet ship, or grain ship, was headed to their desired destination. Seleucia housed a Roman naval fleet, but transportation could be found only on commercial sailing vessels, which sailed more frequently during favorable winds but rather infrequently during fall and winter.

The situation was made more difficult by the presence of pirates, who infested the coasts of the eastern Mediterranean, particularly around Cyprus and Cilicia. One historian of the era noted how pirates had been a problem in the area: "The power of the pirates had its seat in Cilicia at first, and at the outset it was venturesome and elusive; but it took on confidence and boldness during the Mithridatic war, because it lent itself to the king's service. Then, while the Romans were embroiled in civil wars at the gates of Rome, the sea was left unguarded, and gradually drew and enticed them on until they no longer attacked navigators only, but also laid waste islands and maritime cities. And presently men whose wealth gave them power, and those whose lineage was illustrious, and those who laid claim to superior intelligence, began to embark on piratical craft and share their enterprises, feeling that the occupation brought them a certain reputation and distinction. There were also fortified roadsteads and signal-stations for piratical craft in many places, and fleets put in here which were not merely furnished for their peculiar work with sturdy crews, skilful pilots, and light and speedy ships; nay, more annoying than the fear which they inspired was the odious extravagance of their equipment, with their gilded sails, and purple awnings, and silvered oars, as if they rioted in their iniquity and plumed themselves upon it" (Plutarch, *Pompey,* 24). The Roman general Pompey and his successors eradicated many of the pirates in the Mediterranean, but sea travel always faced the threat of piracy and shipwreck.

While waiting for a commercial vessel to take them to Cyprus, Barnabas and Paul may have taught the gospel in Seleucia. Luke was not aware of any success that they had in the city, but he did not join Paul in his travels for another five years or more; he therefore was unaware of many of the details of the first mission (Acts 16:10). Upon their arrival in Salamis on the island of Cyprus, Barnabas and Paul were met by Barnabas's nephew John Mark. Mark's duties are described as being a "minister" to the two disciples (Acts 13:5). Acts 12:12 indicates that "many were gathered" in John Mark's mother's house. This has led to the conclusion that the house was very large and the family quite wealthy, and, therefore, Mark's role may have been to financially assist Barnabas and Paul in their travels. The reason that the group sailed first to Salamis was that it offered a safe harbor; it also served as the rendezvous point for meeting John Mark. The island of Cyprus also had a "faithful" Jewish population to which Barnabas, and possibly John Mark, had ties (Josephus, *Antiquities*, 13.10.4).

PAPHOS

The hurried way in which Luke recounts their arrival in Cyprus and landing in Salamis suggests that the small missionary party had a predetermined itinerary before their arrival. In one phrase, Luke records that "they had gone through the isle unto Paphos," a distance of roughly one hundred miles (Acts 13:6). If the disciples had intended to preach the gospel in whatever cities would accept them, their immediate travel to Paphos is inexplicable. However, an appointment with the Roman proconsul Sergius Paulus in Paphos was sufficient reason to expedite their journey, particularly if they had been delayed at all in their departure from Seleucia.

The beauty of Cyprus lay in her coastlines, which overlook the azure blue waters of the Mediterranean. Traveling along these picturesque coastlines from Salamis to Paphos would have taken the disciples at least a week, giving Paul ample opportunity to acquaint himself with John Mark, whom Barnabas already knew, and at the same time enjoy the coastal scenery.

The island of Cyprus was part of a Roman senatorial province, and the seat of the proconsul was in the city of Paphos, located about sixty stadia away or roughly ten miles from the older pre-Roman city of Paphos. The seat of government included a palatial villa that has been uncovered in modern times (Strabo, *Geography*, 14.6.3). At the time of Barnabas and Paul's visit to the island, the Roman senator Sergius Paulus was living in the governor's palace and welcomed the two disciples to his residence (Acts 13:7). In connection with his record of the visit with Sergius Paulus, Luke introduces Saul's Roman name *Paul* for the first time, where recognition of his Roman citizenship may have been useful (Acts 13:9). Thereafter, Luke uses Paul's Hebrew name exclusively when he recounts his conversion experiences to Aramaic-speaking audiences in Jerusalem and its environs (Acts 22:7, 13; 26:14).

When they met with Sergius Paulus, the proconsul was attended by a Jewish sorcerer whose name was "Bar-jesus" and who made their initial visit more difficult (Acts 13:6). Luke relates that this sorcerer was also known as "Elymas . . . (for so is his name by interpretation)" (Acts 13:8). It thus appears that this particular sorcerer had both a Greek and an Aramaic name. Acts hints at the conversion of Sergius Paulus when it says that Elymas sought "to turn away the deputy from the faith" (Acts 13:8). Luke's portrayal of the conversion of Sergius Paulus is different from that of previous conversions, and now as the missionaries begin to expand into Greek-speaking cities with Greek culture and citizens, we begin to see the emergence of a reasoned conversion rather than the dramatic conversions that took place in Judea and Galilee recorded earlier in Acts.

The pattern that begins to emerge in Paphos is that Paul and his traveling companions are first given an opportunity to present their beliefs either in the local synagogue or publicly, as was the case in Athens, where Paul taught in the shadows of the Parthenon. After hearing the message, their new investigators seem to take time to consider the implications of the missionaries' teachings before they decide whether to be baptized or not. Luke reports that Sergius Paulus was emotionally committed to Barnabas's and Paul's message but not formally committed through baptism so that Elymas could step forward and try to convince the proconsul that their message was false.

To counter the persuasive reasoning of Elymas, Paul rebuked him saying, "O full of all subtilty and all mischief, thou child of the devil, thou enemy of all righteousness, wilt thou not cease to pervert the right ways of the Lord?" (Acts 13:10). Paul inserts into his invective a subtle pun calling Bar-jesus, which literally means "son of Jesus," a son of the devil. For those present, the isolating and marginalizing intent of Paul's statements were clear, and even Sergius Paulus seems to have openly accepted the rebuke of the local sorcerer, who became blind after Paul's rebuke. Sergius Paulus then "believed," but Luke does not record that either he or anyone present was baptized (Acts 13:12). After the public rebuke of Elymas, Barnabas and Paul departed Cyprus for western Asia. Paul never returned to the island in his later missionary travels, nor did he write letters to any branches of the church there, which suggests that this mission to Cyprus did not meet with great success.

ATTALIA

Up to this stage, John Mark had been content to travel with the group. He had traveled across the island of Cyprus and had ministered to the needs of the missionaries, but when Barnabas and Paul set out to cross the Mediterranean between Paphos and the mainland, John Mark headed east and formally departed their company. Luke passes over Mark's departure, saying only that he departed "from them [and] returned to Jerusalem" (Acts 13:13). The brevity of the account may initially give the impression that Mark left on favorable terms. Luke, however, later records that when Paul and Barnabas set out on their second mission the issue of Mark's departure became so heated that the two missionaries departed ways. Barnabas sided with Mark, while Paul is reported to have "thought [it] not good to take him with them, who departed from them from Pamphylia, and went not with them to the work" (Acts 15:38). Whatever reasons Mark gave for his departure, Paul did not feel that they were sufficient. If Mark was indeed supporting the missionaries financially, then his departure would have forced the missionaries to find work while they traveled and taught the gospel, a practice that Paul would observe later but one that is not mentioned during their stay in Cyprus.

With Mark no longer in their company, the small missionary group crossed the Mediterranean Sea to the port city of Attalia, intending to travel inland to some of the larger cities along the established trade routes in the region. The city of Attalia (modern Antalya) is built on a limestone plateau overlooking the Mediterranean. In ancient times it served as a harbor for the inland cities of Perga and Pamphylia and was traversed by a river, which has dried up in modern times due to local irrigation of crops. Attalia was built as a harbor fortress, and the port was locked with a chain, no doubt to keep out pirates and protect commercial vessels. Much of the ancient harbor fortifications are still visible today. Acts does not mention that the missionaries traveled through Attalia on their trip inland, but later Luke records that they passed through Attalia on their way back to Jerusalem, thus suggesting that they were following the well-established trade routes in the region; they therefore would probably have passed through Attalia on both occasions (Acts 14:25). The city was the gateway to Perga, and the disciples could travel overland by foot or sail up the Cestrus River to their destination.

PERGA AND PISIDIAN ANTIOCH

Traveling the short distance from Attalia to Perga would have taken no longer than a day. At Perga, the disciples may have rested a few days prior to traversing the formidable Taurus Mountains. By ancient standards, Perga's grandeur was comparable to Ephesus. The city contained a massive theater that would seat fourteen thousand observers and, like Ephesus, housed a temple of Artemis.

Luke's only clue that Barnabas and Paul taught the gospel in Perga is found in his statement, "But when they *departed from*

Perga." If they had only passed through he likely would have stated "and passing" through Perga, as he did in other instances (Acts 13:14; 16:8). Up to this point, the missionaries had approached mainly Gentiles, with the exception of the Jewish sorcerer Elymas. Perhaps their earlier experiences had led them to believe that a mission to Gentiles would go well; however, Luke records no baptisms prior to their arrival in Antioch. Several individuals had expressed interest in their message, but none appear to have been baptized.

This subtle hint may reveal why Barnabas and Paul, upon reaching Antioch in Pisidia, immediately sought out the local synagogue and preached there on the Jewish Sabbath (Saturday). After listening to the reading of the law and the prophets, as was customary in a Jewish worship meeting, Paul asked for an opportunity to speak to the audience. His audience on that day was comprised of "Men of Israel, and ye that fear God"—or Jews and converts to Judaism (Acts 13:16). Paul testified that Jesus Christ was the promised Messiah, whose death and resurrection had been foretold by prophets (Acts 13:17–41). Paul's tone was neither condemning nor condescending, but instead reveals the logical progression of how Paul came to know that Jesus was the Christ. He testified that Jesus fulfilled the promise given to David that through his lines the Messiah would be born (2 Samuel 7:12, 29; Isaiah 11:1), that he would be slain for the sins of the world (Isaiah 53:4–9), and that he would be raised from the dead so that he would not taste corruption (Psalm 16:10). Behind this reasoned speech is the man who earlier had taught that Jesus could not be viewed as the fulfillment of the prophecies of the coming Messiah. During the long months and years he spent in Arabia, Tarsus, and Antioch, Paul came to know more deeply that Jesus was truly the Christ. Not only had he seen him personally, but he was now convinced that the prophets had seen him as well.

Imbedded in Paul's speech is a hint at his own experience on the road to Damascus. In his later epistles he recounted the experience openly, but here he makes only a passing reference to it. Paul taught that the resurrected Jesus "was seen many days of them which came up with him from Galilee to Jerusalem, who are his witnesses unto the people. And *we* declare unto you glad tidings" (Acts 13:31–32; emphasis added). Paul here differentiates his own experience on the road to Damascus from the experience of Jesus' Galilean disciples, who were called as "witnesses unto the people." When coupled with the fact that Paul does not refer to himself as an apostle during his mission with Barnabas, it becomes apparent that Paul had not been ordained an apostle at this time was not a member of the Quorum of the Twelve.

Paul's speech in Antioch in Pisidia was warmly received by the Gentiles who had been attracted to Judaism but who had never become full converts. Acts reports that "the Gentiles besought that these words might be preached to them the next sabbath" (Acts 13:42). In retelling this part of the story, Luke records that "the next sabbath day came almost the whole city together to hear the word of God. But when the Jews saw the multitudes, they were filled with envy" (Acts 13:44–45). That envy may have stemmed from the fact that Barnabas and Paul were drawing in huge crowds, while the local leaders did not. Or, if Barnabas and Paul used the synagogue as a forum to deliver their first message, and then began to meet elsewhere, taking the typical synagogue attender with them, that also would have incited envy. In that case, the local Jewish leaders would have felt taken advantage of because they opened their synagogue to Barnabas and Paul, who then led some of their congregation away.

There was also another element at work. Those with whom Barnabas and Paul had their initial success appear to have been

Gentiles, for as Luke reports, "the whole city" came to hear the word, which would certainly indicate many more than the local members of the synagogue. The envy of the Jews in such a situation is understandable—they were seeing this new Christian message being taught in their synagogues by their fellow countrymen to Jews—and to any who were attending synagogue services because of an interest in converting to Judaism. Luke records an important development in Antioch when he reports that "the Jews stirred up the devout and honourable women, and the chief men of the city, and raised persecution against Paul and Barnabas, and expelled them out of their coasts" (Acts 13:50). The conversion of gentile women to Judaism became almost proverbial, because unlike the men they could simply believe and were not required to undergo anything similar to circumcision. Luke thus reports that the honorable women of the city, with whom the Jewish leaders could find an audience, were able to exert their influence on the town leaders, likely their husbands, and have Barnabas and Paul run out of town.

Luke, who authored his gospel prior to writing Acts, left a subtle hint that their mission in Pisidian Antioch had been very much like the mission of the Seventy. Before sending out the Seventy, Jesus instructed them saying, "But into whatsoever city ye enter, and they receive you not, go your ways out into the streets of the same, and say, Even the very dust of your city, which cleaveth on us, we do wipe off against you" (Luke 10:10–11). Luke adds at the end of their stay in Pisidian Antioch that Barnabas and Paul, "shook off the dust of their feet against them, and came unto Iconium" (Acts 13:51). The suggestion is that like the Seventy during the mortal ministry of Jesus, who were sent out without "purse, nor scrip" (Luke 10:4), and who were also commanded to shake the dust from their feet when they were rejected, Barnabas and Paul were similarly rejected and were forced to go to Iconium.

ICONIUM, LYSTRA, DERBE

The trip between Antioch in Pisidia and Iconium is roughly eighty miles and would take roughly one week to complete. The terrain is rather mountainous but gently gives way to lush and fertile inland valleys. While traveling on one of the main roads between western Asia and the commercial centers of the eastern Levant, Barnabas and Paul would have arrived at the thriving trade center of Iconium (modern Konya) after an exhausting climb through the rugged Taurus Mountains.

In 25 B.C., Iconium was incorporated into the Roman province of Galatia, and although it was not the capital city of the region, it was certainly one of the most populous and prosperous. When Marco Polo later visited the city he claimed that they produced the best carpets in the region. If Barnabas and Paul were lacking funds, Iconium would have provided excellent opportunities for temporary employment.

As they had done in Antioch in Pisidia, Barnabas and Paul attended the local synagogue meetings, where they were given the opportunity to speak. Iconium, however, proved more difficult for the missionaries. As Luke reports, "the unbelieving Jews stirred up the Gentiles, and made their minds evil affected against the brethren" (Acts 14:2). Luke then adds that in Iconium, presumably as a contrast to the practice in other cities, the missionaries stayed a "long time" (Acts 14:3). Their reasons for staying longer in Iconium are not given, but the statement is surprising since Luke has just described their reception as less than favorable. The reasons for their stay may indeed be linked to John Mark's departure, who left them before they landed at Attalia and before their trip to Pisidian Antioch—and who, as noted earlier, may have been helping to support their mission.

These small enclosures represent the remains of ancient storefronts where the missionaries could seek temporary employment while they stayed in the city and taught the gospel. Luke records that Barnabas and Paul gathered a large following in this city [Pisidian Antioch], but eventually faced severe persecution from local Jews. Luke's lengthy account of the missionaries' stay in the city may suggest that they remained there for an extended period of time (Acts 13:14–52).

Since they were traveling without "purse, nor scrip," and since John Mark had left them, Barnabas and Paul may have found themselves without food or money in an environment where there were few believers. The "long time" that Luke used to describe their stay in Iconium was almost certainly mandated by the need to earn money for the remainder of their mission.

Their continued preaching in Iconium ultimately led to a division in the city, "and part held with the Jews, and part with the apostles" (Acts 14:4). The parallel construction of the phrase gives the appearance that the division was down the middle, but the very next verse indicates that the Jews and the Gentiles plotted together to assault and stone the disciples (Acts 14:5). If the congregation of Jews and gentile followers were equally divided over whether to accept the disciples, then we would naturally expect that some defense of the missionaries

Overlooking a small stream and lush farmlands, the city of Lystra remains undisturbed today. The city was home to one of Paul's most beloved missionary companions—Timothy. Some of the first Christian baptisms, including Timothy and his mother's, were likely performed in this small stream.

would be presented. However, the Jews were able to persuade "their rulers" to take action against the missionaries (Acts 14:5). Barnabas and Paul were made aware of the intentions of their enemies and fled to Lystra and Derbe (Acts 14:6).

Associated with the city of Iconium is the only known description of Paul's physical appearance from the ancient world. According to the legendary or pseudepigraphical work *The Acts of Paul,* "a man named Onesiphorus, who had heard that Paul was come to Iconium, went out with his children Simmias and Zeno and his wife Lectra to meet Paul, that he might receive him to his house. For Titus had told him what Paul looked like. For (hitherto) he had not seen him in the flesh, but only in the spirit. And he went along the royal road which leads to Lystra, and stood there waiting for him, and looked at (all) who came, according to Titus's description. And he saw Paul coming, a man small of stature, with a bald head and crooked legs, in a good state of body, with eyebrows meeting and nose somewhat hooked, full of friendliness; for now he appeared like a man, and now he had the face of an angel" (*Acts of Paul,* 3.2). The description of Paul when he visited Iconium may have been preserved through legend and clearly depicts him at a later stage in life, but it also appears to preserve some historical fact since its less than flattering portrayal would hardly be the substance of forgery.

The distance between Iconium and Lystra is roughly sixteen miles, making Lystra nearly one hundred miles from Pisidian Antioch. The city was founded as a Roman colony in 26 B.C. by Augustus, and many veterans of the Roman army had retired there. The Italian settlers appear to have dominated civic affairs, since nearly all the inscriptions that have been found on the site are written in Latin. Native to the region were the Lycian tribes, who spoke a dialect (Lycaonian) that was distantly related to Phrygian. Strategically located on the western road that led through the Cilician Gates back to Tarsus and the coast, the city had long been used as a base camp for Roman campaigns against the Taurus tribes in the region.

In Lystra, the two missionaries would have encountered indigenous Lycians who had been assimilated into the Greco-Roman culture of the region but who had very few contacts with Judaism. Unlike in his record of the previous cities of central Asia, Luke mentions no Jewish synagogue in the city. Paul, who appears to have preached openly in the market in Lystra, healed a man who had been unable to walk since his birth (Acts 14:8–11). The healing touched off a flurry of activity in the marketplace, where a group of local Lycians gathered to worship Barnabas and Paul as Zeus and Hermes respectively (Acts 14:12–13). The reason the local population assumed that the two disciples were manifestations of their local deities might be found in the images of Zeus originating from the region of Lystra, which show an elderly Zeus attended by a younger assistant. Their assumption that Barnabas was Zeus supports the understanding that Barnabas was both older than Paul and the senior figure of the two.

The two disciples, whom Luke now calls apostles for the first time, heard of the attempt to deify them and quickly put a stop to the proceedings, and their method of doing so reveals something of their character. When they heard of the local attempts to worship them, "they rent their clothes, and ran in among the people" (Acts 14:14). Their reaction was a culturally conditioned response, first mentioned in the Old Testament when Reuben returned to find that his brother Joseph was not in the pit where they had placed him, which caused him to rend his clothes (Genesis 37:29). Reuben reported the incident to his father Jacob, who also "rent his clothes" as a sign of mourning (Genesis 37:34). A report from a later rabbinic text reports that when blasphemy is heard, "the judges stand on their feet and tear their clothing, and never sew them back up" (Bavli Sanhedrin, 7:5). In the recorded cases of the rending of clothing, the context is usually that of mourning or refusing to accept the facts that have been presented. In this instance, Barnabas and Paul reacted vehemently to being worshipped, and the rending of their clothes was a clear sign of their refusal to accept such an honor. But their reaction was also overtly Jewish, which the local population did not seem to understand.

Their impassioned plea to the local congregation, as Luke records, "scarce restrained" the local population from worshipping them (Acts 14:18). Had they been among Jews, the act of rending their clothes would have been a sign sufficient enough to demonstrate that they would refuse such honor. However, the locals changed their minds only when they learned that Barnabas and Paul were indeed "men of like passions with you, and preach unto you that ye should turn from these vanities unto the living God" (Acts 14:15).

As these events transpired in the marketplace, certain Jews

from Pisidian Antioch were traveling towards Lystra to apprehend Barnabas and Paul. Along the way, these antagonists from Pisidian Antioch enlisted help from the men of Iconium. Their trip to apprehend the two missionaries took them over a distance of one hundred miles, a testimony to their determination and hatred. When the mob arrived they persuaded the citizens of Lystra to join them, then apprehended and stoned Paul, leaving him for dead (Acts 14:19). It remains unclear why Barnabas was not treated similarly. Surprisingly, Paul and Barnabas later returned to all three places from which the mobs had originated—Pisidian Antioch, Iconium, and Lystra—a significant testimony to their courage and commitment to their message.

After Paul had revived, he traveled with Barnabas to Derbe, where Luke records that they taught the gospel. A later traveling companion of Paul's, Gaius, came from Derbe; it is possible that Paul met Gaius for the first time on this initial trip to Gaius's hometown (Acts 20:4). The brevity with which Luke relates their stay in Derbe indicates that they were not well received, and therefore they departed immediately.

THE RETURN TRIP TO ANTIOCH

Two features stand out during the return trip through the cities they had visited and their return to the city of their departure—Antioch. First, the missionaries "ordained . . . elders in every church" and second, Luke refers to Barnabas and Paul as apostles (Acts 14:23; see also 14:14). Surprisingly, Luke does not record a single baptism during the first missionary journey, even though he does recount that several audiences believed the words of the disciples. The mission may have been more successful in converting Paul or convincing others that his conversion was genuine than it was in converting the multitudes. Paul's subsequent visits to the region on his second and third missionary journeys illustrate that he had great hopes to find souls willing to be baptized, but for some reason Luke gives the impression that few, if any, baptisms took place on this missionary journey. (Those who were ordained elders may well have converted earlier.)

As mentioned earlier, one of the most troubling obstacles to conversion between A.D. 30 and 49 was the requirement that all males who joined the church had to undergo circumcision, which likely became a significant obstacle on this mission. By contrast, at the beginning of Paul's next mission, after the issue of circumcision had been resolved through the decision of a church council, Luke records, "*she* [Lydia] was baptized, *and her household*" (Acts 16:15; emphasis added). The later missionary journeys, unlike the mission with Barnabas, were punctuated by gentile baptisms, a subtle hint by Luke that the first mission was much more difficult than the account of it would initially suggest.

The ordaining of "elders" in every church may also warrant closer attention. If indeed the work was impeded by the issue of circumcision of gentile converts, then those who were left to administer to the needs of the fledgling church in the region were almost certainly Jews. This of itself is not an issue, but every instance of persecution during the mission with Barnabas is Jewish in origin; this raises the issue that after the departure of the missionaries old enemies would be able to influence and perhaps corrupt their countrymen who had formerly been of the same faith. During this mission Jewish antagonism toward the missionaries had been so strong as to thwart their efforts in several cities, as well as resulting in the stoning of Paul. With resistance to the gospel message being so intense, how well would new converts stand up to it?

Moreover, several of the cities appear to have had no Jewish presence at all, the result of which may have been that

Barnabas and Paul were unable to establish a congregation that was sufficiently strong to weather the storms after their departure. This is particularly true of the cities of Lystra and Derbe, which are the first two cities mentioned by name in Paul's next missionary journey (Acts 16:1). When Barnabas and Paul reported their doings to the brethren in Antioch, "they rehearsed all that God had done with them, and how he had opened the door of faith unto the Gentiles" (Acts 14:27). How many Gentiles actually came through that door remains a difficult question to answer, but certainly the door was now open, and as Acts makes clear, the church leaders would need to decide the issue of how to proceed in the gentile areas of the church.

In Luke's summary of this mission, he reports favorably that Paul and Barnabas called "the church together" and reported "all that God had done with them," which in English is difficult to interpret and may reveal the phraseology of a Semitic source (Acts 14:27). Although we could quite naturally understand the phrase to mean "through us," one early text alters the phrase to read, "all that God had done with their souls," pointing out that the success of the first mission was not only that the Gentiles believed, but also that God had perfected the souls of Barnabas and Paul (Codex Bezae, fifth century). This altered reading narrows the focus to the character or personality of Barnabas and Paul, who had undergone an amazing transformation that was now recognizable to all. Paul had now manifestly proved to the local congregation that his conversion was genuine. The great success of the mission with Barnabas was likely twofold: it convincingly demonstrated that Gentiles believed in the gospel message and it showed that Paul was sincere in his conversion, willing to suffer persecution for the name of Christ.

Luke uses the term apostle to refer to Barnabas and Paul only in Acts 14:4, 14. Paul is nowhere else referred to as an apostle by Luke, suggesting that the question of whether or not Paul was an apostle was a concern even in the first century. Some scribes have corrected the verses in Acts 14 so that they do not explicitly call Paul or Barnabas apostles. On the other hand, Paul was unequivocal in calling himself an apostle on numerous occasions (see, for example, Galatians 1:1). One possibility is that Luke mistakenly called Paul an apostle before his call, reflecting back into the historical record what later became reality. Unfortunately, none of Paul's surviving correspondence can be definitively dated prior to the Jerusalem conference (A.D. 49), which might indicate whether Paul called himself an apostle at any time during the first missionary journey.

After the death of Judas Iscariot, the eleven apostles met in Jerusalem to call another apostle to fill the vacancy left by Judas. When they met they set forth the requirements for all future apostles, stating, "Wherefore of these men which have companied with us all the time that the Lord Jesus went in and out among us, beginning from the baptism of John, unto that same day that he was taken up from us, must one be ordained to be a witness with us of his resurrection" (Acts 1:21–22). Two requirements were thus established: first, the new disciple had to be a follower of Jesus from the time of John the Baptist, and second, he had to be a witness of the resurrection of Jesus. This decision effectively limited the pool of potential apostles as later generations of Christians misunderstood the original deliberations of the brethren in Jerusalem. The initial considerations of the surviving eleven apostles likely included everyone who was worthy to be called to that office; however, as they sought to limit the pool of potential candidates, they observed the above criteria as they singled out two men who fulfilled both requirements. Later generations of church leaders would mistakenly shift the stewardship of the apostles onto the shoulders of the bishops because there were no longer any men alive who had followed Jesus from the time of John's baptism and who were witnesses of the resurrection.

This decision ultimately led to an extreme reverence for the eyewitness generation, particularly those who had known Jesus and John the Baptist. However, it is a misunderstanding to suppose that the original Quorum of Twelve Apostles intended their decision to limit the calling of all future apostles. Nevertheless, even in Paul's day he distinguishes between the Quorum of the Twelve and other apostles: "Cephas, then of the twelve" and "James; then of all the apostles" (1 Corinthians 15:5, 7). For Paul, and other early Christian authors, the term *apostle* could refer to those who fit the two criteria announced in Acts 1 when the first new apostle was called, and it could also refer to those who were specifically members of the Quorum of the Twelve. Later epistles of Paul would reveal that many discounted his apostolic calling because, unlike the original apostles, he was not a follower of Jesus from the time of John's baptism, although he certainly was a witness of the resurrected Savior.

The fact that Luke called Barnabas and Paul apostles should be considered more than a random error, where later facts were inserted into an earlier historical time period. Luke first mentions that the people of the city of Iconium were divided, "and part held with the Jews, and part with the apostles" (Acts 14:4). This general reference may have nothing to do with Barnabas and Paul holding the office of apostle, but may indicate that the two missionaries were in line with or represented the position of the apostles in Jerusalem. The Jews of the city were divided in their allegiance, but Barnabas and Paul were not, an important historical note for Paul, who was being given an opportunity to turn back to his old ways and follow his Pharisaic training. Luke may be subtly hinting that Paul stayed firm in the faith on the side of the apostles.

The second reference to Barnabas and Paul being apostles is clear grammatically: "Which when the apostles, Barnabas and Paul, heard" (Acts 14:14). Unfortunately, the reference has been taken as a mistake for centuries, and some of the earliest Christian scribes of the New Testament removed the noun *apostles* to offer what they felt was a clarification of the text. One text completely removes Paul's name from the reference to show that Barnabas but not Paul was an apostle. At the heart of the issue is the fact that at this early stage all of the apostles from Jesus' ministry in Jerusalem were likely still alive (except Judas, who had been replaced by Matthias); the addition of Barnabas or Paul to that quorum in the mid-40s would therefore have been an impossibility. Perhaps, as in the early days of our current dispensation, apostles were called who were never members of the Quorum of Twelve, making Barnabas and Paul traveling apostles similar in status to General Authorities. Or Paul and Barnabas may have been apostles in the sense that they were indeed "witness with [the apostles] of his resurrection" (Acts 1:22). Luke may have been trying to intimate that Paul should, like all other living witnesses of the resurrection, be considered an apostle. Later, when certain opponents of Paul attempted to discount his ministry and apostleship, Paul applied the term to himself by definition rather than as a member of the Quorum. If Luke were a traveling companion of Paul, he would most likely reflect the same understanding and usage of the term.

CONCLUSION

The missionary journey of Barnabas, Paul, and for a short while John Mark reveals more about the dynamics of the church and its gradual development than it does about how many joined the church. Paul was given his first opportunity to show his determination to a wider audience and to show that his conversion was sincere. In that regard, the mission may have been more about Paul than about the branches of the church. Barnabas, although the likely leader of this mission, immediately fades into the background and becomes somewhat of a secondary figure throughout the remainder of the New Testament.

Interwoven throughout this mission are the themes of difficulty and limited success. Many believed in Paul's words and accepted the words of Jesus Christ on an emotional level, but Luke does not record any physical response to Paul's teachings. The account of the mission with Barnabas does not contain a single example of a baptism being performed. At the end of his journey, Paul traveled back through the areas of his mission and ordained elders to oversee the branches, but those whom he ordained may have converted prior to Paul's visit; Paul may have simply been organizing them into branches following instructions he had received from the leaders of the church in Jerusalem. Luke's report certainly makes this a viable conclusion.

A closer look at Paul during the first mission reveals a new missionary who was beginning to take the lead in discussions and mentally formulate careful responses to outside attacks. Luke also shows that on several occasions, Paul presented his message using the Old Testament exclusively. The New Testament had not been written at the time of this mission, and, interestingly, Luke does not make any reference to Paul quoting from the words of Jesus directly at this stage, although later Paul would do so (Acts 20:35). Paul, Luke's personal hero, is depicted in terms that are entirely favorable, concluding with Luke's climactic touch that Paul should be considered an apostle. Luke never stated that Paul's authority was equal to that of the Quorum of the Twelve but only that Paul's personal witness was equal in power.

Chapter 5

THE JERUSALEM CONFERENCE

"The real reason for the martyrdom of such men as Paul and Peter was this: The world, while willing to believe, in part, what God had revealed, was not willing to accept a new revelation, for which the former revelation was intended to prepare them."
—Orson F. Whitney

After Paul and Barnabas returned to Antioch from their mission, they gave a report of their efforts to the saints there, telling them that God "had opened the door of faith unto the Gentiles" (Acts 14:27). Having made their report, "they abode long time with the disciples" (Acts 14:28). This "long time" that Luke refers to represents the final months of Paul's fourteen-year period between his first visit with Peter in Jerusalem and his return there in Acts 15. He had stayed away from the turmoil that was brewing in Jerusalem, first teaching the gospel in his hometown and eventually teaming with Barnabas to visit Cyprus and several cities of central Asia. Paul's activity as a persecutor had slowly faded into the past, and while his name would forever be associated with the stoning of Stephen and anti-Christian activities in Jerusalem, he had proven that his conversion to the gospel was genuine and sincere.

Word of Paul's missionary activities in Asia slowly reached Jerusalem, where a hard-line faction within the church began to contend against those who had taught the gospel to Gentiles. Their teaching that "except ye be circumcised after the manner of Moses, ye cannot be saved" (Acts 15:1) was certainly a response to the missionary activity of Paul and Barnabas among the Gentiles. Their response also indicates that prior to the mission of Paul and Barnabas, very few Gentiles had been taught the gospel and fewer still had converted. With the potential that many Gentiles might accept the gospel and join themselves to the faith, an opposition faction tried to bar their entrance by requiring that all male members must first be circumcised (Acts 15:1, 5). Paul and Barnabas, who seem to have feared that the decision would be made in favor of the hard-liners, traveled to Jerusalem to represent the Gentiles.

Peter presided over the conference, which took place in Jerusalem in A.D. 49. The account in Acts 15:1–35, however, raises serious questions about the development of the early church in Jerusalem—or perhaps the disintegration of the early church. Luke mentions that the initial complaint about the Gentiles was made to "the brethren" in Antioch and that the "apostles and elders" in Jerusalem were called to hear the case (Acts 15:1, 6). Luke then inserts into this positive picture the statement, "there rose up certain of the sect of the Pharisees which believed, saying, That it was needful to circumcise them [Gentiles], and to command them to keep the law of Moses" (Acts 15:5).

Luke's account makes it clear that those who taught that all male members must be circumcised were from Judea, and that they had intentionally traveled to Antioch to correct the problem raised by Paul and Barnabas and others who were teaching the gospel to Gentiles. The teaching of these brethren from Judea must have carried some weight among members in

Antioch because Jerusalem had been the center of the church up to this time. Luke is not clear on who these representatives from Judea were and who sent them to issue these directions. The message of these Judean representatives touched off a heated debate in Antioch, or as Luke reports, "no small dissension and disputation with them [the Judean representatives]" (Acts 15:2). Among the members in Antioch, Paul and Barnabas particularly disputed the authenticity of this message and determined to travel to Jerusalem to discern what the leaders of the church had revealed on the matter.

Shortly after their arrival a meeting was called, where Peter was designated as the presiding church authority (Acts 15:6–12; Galatians 2:9). Luke loosely refers to the presence of apostles, but does not list any of them by name (Acts 15:2, 4, 6). James, the brother of Jesus was also present (Acts 15:13), but no members of the original Quorum of Twelve Apostles are mentioned except for Peter. James the brother of John the Beloved had already died under the persecution of Herod Agrippa 1 (c. A.D. 44). It is likely that many members of the original Twelve were still alive, even though Luke does not specifically mention them as present in Jerusalem for the conference. Moreover, Luke's sources for the event led him to state that "certain [members] of the sect of the Pharisees" also attended the conference and felt that they had something to contribute (Acts 15:5). If the lines between Judaism and Christianity were as clearly drawn in Jerusalem as they were in other places (Antioch), the presence of a faction referred to as Pharisees within the church is problematic. If, however, the lines between the two were not as distinct in Jerusalem, then they might have felt that insistence to the principles and commandments of the law of Moses might bring these wayward Jews (Peter, James, Barnabas, and Paul) back into the true Messianic fold and further exclude Gentiles from wanting to join with them.

Historically, the members of the church in Jerusalem, unlike other branches of the church in gentile cities, were slow to accept the conversion of Gentiles and welcome them into full fellowship. Luke is clear on two details of the story; first, that Peter presided over the proceedings, and second, that Peter was firm on the direction that should be taken. These comforting details offer some solace in an otherwise difficult situation.

The hard-line Pharisaic faction in the church likely had its origins in the deliberations of the Sanhedrin during Jesus' mortal ministry. On several occasions the Gospels report that the Sanhedrin, which was dominated by Sadducees, had difficulty reaching a decision on how to respond to Jesus and his followers. The Gospel of John records that Caiaphas rebuked some members of the Sanhedrin, telling them that "ye know nothing at all," implying that their hesitancy to deal with Jesus was informed by ignorance (John 11:49). Toleration of Jesus, Caiaphas concluded, was tantamount to allowing the Romans to come and take away their nation and their ability to rule themselves (John 11:50). An earlier episode shows that Nicodemus, traditionally thought to be a Pharisee, defended Jesus to the Sanhedrin and for doing so was reviled by them (John 7:50–53). These dissensions led to a fractured Sanhedrin that in many ways represented a fractured Jewish people, who either accepted and worshipped Jesus or cast him aside as a fraud.

Luke specifically mentions complaints about gentile converts from members who were Pharisees. These Pharisees may have been nothing more than sympathizers, who believed in Jesus but were unwilling to see that his teachings laid the foundation for a religion apart from Judaism. As long as Christianity remained in close stride with traditional Judaism, these Pharisees felt a sense of belonging. Like the "elders and apostles" in Jerusalem, the Pharisaic believers wanted their positions voiced also.

Another startling aspect of the Jerusalem conference is the presence of James, the brother of Jesus, who at the time appears to be an authority of similar standing to Peter (Acts 15:13). The early date of the Jerusalem conference (A.D. 49) almost certainly precludes James holding any senior role in the Quorum of the Twelve, but he could have filled the vacancy left by the death of James the son of Zebedee. James, the brother of Jesus, according to early church tradition, was the first bishop of the city of Jerusalem, a fact that may explain his role in the Jerusalem conference, which was being held in his hometown. Eusebius records, "The throne of James—who was the first to receive from the Saviour and His apostles the episcopacy [bishopric] of the Jerusalem church, and was called Christ's brother, as the sacred books show—has been preserved to this day [mid-fourth century A.D.]" (*Church History*, 7.19). Taking a lead from early church tradition, it is almost certain that James's role in the Jerusalem conference was to represent the local branch(es) of the church in the city; James's statements would therefore be an important witness to what was going on among the members in Jerusalem.

The calling of James as an apostle has been assumed in modern times, but he nowhere refers to himself as such. Paul, who uses the definition of an apostle derived from Acts 1:21–22, states that Jesus showed himself to "Cephas, then of the twelve: After that, he was seen of above five hundred brethren at once; of whom the greater part remain unto this present, but some are fallen asleep. After that, he was seen of James; then of all the apostles" (1 Corinthians 15:5–7). Paul, who also calls himself an apostle, clearly distinguishes between the Quorum of Twelve Apostles and those who were considered apostles according to the definition set forth in Acts 1. James, who was not a follower of Jesus during the mortal ministry (John 7:3–5), was considered an apostle because he had known Jesus since the baptism of John and had become a witness to the resurrection, an event that likely coincided with his conversion. Understanding James's role in the Jerusalem conference may be more important than understanding Peter's, whose role is quite clear, since he was both the president of the church and the presiding priesthood authority.

THE FAMILY OF JESUS IN THE EARLY CHURCH

The Gospel of Mark records that Jesus had four brothers and at least two sisters: "James, and Joses, and of Juda, and Simon? and are not his sisters here with us?" (Mark 6:3). The Gospel of Matthew, written slightly later than Mark's, records that Jesus' brothers were "James, and Joses, and Simon, and Judas" (Matthew 13:55). Unfortunately, modern translations have obscured the fact that Matthew names Jesus' second brother "Joseph," instead of "Joses" as Mark does. Joses was a common Greek form of the Hebrew name Joseph; clearly Matthew was aware of Jesus' brothers from personal acquaintance or from Aramaic sources. The four brothers of Jesus were antagonistic toward Jesus during his lifetime, but records show that they gathered with their mother in the upper room shortly after the resurrection (Acts 1:14). Tradition suggests that they all became followers of Jesus and exerted considerable influence in Judea and Galilee after his death.

Hegesippus, an early church historian, reports on the Lord's family, saying, "And there still survived of the Lord's family the grandsons of Jude, who was said to be His brother, humanly speaking. These were informed against as being of David's line, and brought by the evocatus before Domitian Caesar, who was as of the advent of Christ as Herod had been. Domitian asked them whether they were descended from David, and they admitted it. . . . When asked about Christ and His kingdom—what it was like, and where and when it would appear—they explained that it was not of this world. . . . On hearing this, Domitian found no fault with them, but despising them as beneath his notice let them go free and issued orders terminating the persecution of the Church. On their release *they became leaders of the churches,* both because they had borne testimony and *because they were of the Lord's family*" (Eusebius, *Church History,* 3.20; emphasis added). Even as late as the mid-second century A.D. the memory that Jesus' brothers served in positions of leadership in or around Jerusalem was still prevalent. Moreover, tradition preserved some remembrance that the brothers were accorded special status because of their relationship to Jesus.

Other relatives of the Lord are also mentioned in the writings of Hegesippus, who says, "Consequently they came and presided over every church, as being martyrs and members of the Lord's family, and since profound peace came to every church they survived till the reign of Trajan Caesar—till the son of the Lord's uncle, the aforesaid Simon son of Clopas, was similarly informed against by the heretical sects and brought up on the same charge before Atticus, the provincial governor" (Eusebius, *Church History,* 3.32). Again, the tradition that the Lord's immediate family members were granted special status is prevalent, including the tradition that they were given callings of leadership in or around Judea.

Jesus himself descended from a strong Jewish family with strong historical ties to the house of David and the city of David, Bethlehem. Those ties would have been equally strong for his family members, who as late as the second century were still recognized as legitimate heirs to the throne of David. James, the brother of Jesus who was closest to him in age, was the first member of the family to hold an important calling in the church, and part of his prestige and authority were derived from his close family connections to his older brother.

His presence at the Jerusalem conference is therefore vitally important for two reasons. First, he was likely the highest ecclesiastical authority in the city of Jerusalem after the apostles, and second, his family connections earned him considerable authority in Jewish circles that had converted to Christianity, including the hard-line Pharisees who believed in Jesus but were unwilling to accept Gentiles into the church.

THE DECISION OF THE JERUSALEM CONFERENCE

Peter, as president of the church, presided over the decision issued by the Jerusalem council, while James, a man of immense authority and prestige, was (according to tradition) present to represent the Jerusalem branch(es) as well as bring hard-line Pharisees into line with the inspired decision that would be issued. As Acts relates the story, Peter stated unequivocally that the Lord had revealed to him how the gospel would go forth to the Gentiles. He taught the assembly, "Ye know how that a good while ago God made choice among us, that the Gentiles by my mouth should hear the word of the gospel, and believe. And God, which knoweth the hearts, bare them witness, giving them the Holy Ghost, even as he did unto us; and put no difference between us and them, purifying their hearts by faith. Now therefore why tempt ye God, to put a yoke upon the neck of the disciples, which neither our fathers nor we were able to bear? But we believe that through the grace of the Lord Jesus Christ we shall be saved, even as they" (Acts 15:7–11). Embedded in Peter's remark is a subtle rebuke, phrased rhetorically, "Why tempt ye God?" Luke, who was not present on that day but whose sources provided an account of its proceedings, does not indicate any reaction to Peter's words, except silence (Acts 15:12).

Given that Peter was the ranking priesthood authority on the earth at the time, and that those in attendance were Christians—although some in attendance were certainly Jewish Christians with Pharisaic leanings—it is surprising that the decision to no longer require circumcision for Gentiles was not immediately issued after Peter's testimony. Luke records that Barnabas and Paul were given opportunity to speak immediately following Peter's remarks and permitted to relate their experiences in the gentile cities of the Mediterranean, a report that clearly supported the prior witness and testimony that God was making bare his arm in the eyes of the Gentiles. Although Luke was not aware of any dissensions in the meeting, his account seems to imply that upon hearing the testimony of Barnabas and Paul, some in the crowd rejected their testimony because, as Luke reports, James then stood to settle the issue, saying, "Men and brethren, hearken unto me: Simeon hath declared how God at the first did visit the Gentiles" (Acts 15:13–14). James's statement shows that he was not addressing the leading brethren, since he did not direct his comments to Peter or the apostles generally, but instead was addressing himself to the brethren of the crowd. Moreover, he referred to Peter using his Hebrew name Simon/Simeon rather than his Greek name, indicating that his audience was a local gathering of Aramaic-speaking Christians who almost certainly had at least national ties to the hard-line Pharisees present. If James's words are not understood in this context, then by implication his statements are given as a correction of Peter's testimony, which could be inferred from his statement, "but rather listen to me," a conclusion that seems entirely unlikely (Acts 15:13; author's translation).

James, realizing that the crowd would hearken to his words because of his position and family connections, then taught them, using the words of the pre-exilic prophet Amos, that the salvation of the Gentiles had been foretold in scripture (Acts 15:16–17; Amos 9:11–12). After his introductory comments, James issued "his" decision, which should not be taken as a counter to the decision of Peter but rather in support of it—and given in humble recognition that the keys of the kingdom were in Peter's hands even though the crowd also looked to the authority of James (Acts 15:19).

The wording of the decision is couched in awkward language: "My sentence is, that we trouble not them, which from among the Gentiles are turned to God: But that we write unto them, that they abstain from pollutions of idols, and from fornication, and from things strangled, and from blood" (Acts 15:19–20). In modern English, James's statement, "my sentence is," places his recommendation in the context of a judicial decision that is handed out as a sentence or punishment. Luke's wording, however, can indicate the ideas of "considering, feeling, thinking, or discerning," all suggesting that a person has had all the facts placed before him or her and is now in a position to make a choice or render a decision. Luke's account implies that James was looked to as the authority who should issue the decision, but James's statement more likely was intended to be a public recognition of Peter's testimony instead of the harsher English translation that suggests James both issued the council's decision and that it was given as a punishment.

James's statement, given its current context, appears to be a brokered decision to keep the hard-line faction of the church from dissenting and leaving the church altogether. The real issue that the council was convened to resolve was whether or not Gentiles needed to observe the commandment to be circumcised, but prior to James's statements the discussion had focused more on whether there were any Gentiles who believed. Peter, Barnabas, and Paul all testified that God had poured out his Spirit upon the Gentiles, and that many of them had become followers of Jesus Christ. James equally testified that God had revealed the time when the Gentiles would also become a covenant people. This direction was certainly in opposition to that proposed by the hardliners: "Except ye be circumcised after the manner of Moses, ye cannot be saved" (Acts 15:1). James then added an important injunction aimed at pacifying his more rigorous brethren in Judea. Had the council simply issued a decision regarding the question of circumcision, it appears that the church could have been permanently fractured between the older Jewish converts with Pharisaic leanings and the few gentile converts who were now hearkening to the call of the missionaries. The number of Gentiles in the church was insufficient to withstand such a division, while the Jewish mission had always been plagued by opposition and persecution.

The council further agreed that Paul and Barnabas would travel to Antioch with two representatives from the Judean branches, Judas Barsabas and Silas, to confirm the council's decision and also to avoid any schism that might result if only Paul and Barnabas reported back. These representatives carried letters with them stating the decision, which in the ancient world was the most authoritative way to disseminate information (but as later New Testament writings will show, such letters were also easily forged and corrupted). The council further recognized that "we have heard, that certain which went out from us have troubled you with words, subverting your souls" (Acts 15:24). Public recognition of Judean missionaries who had taught circumcision was designed to forestall further divisions in the branches and also make it clear that the council would communicate through authorized priesthood representatives. The council disparaged misguided attempts at steadying the ark by referring to those who made decisions requiring circumcision as those "to whom we gave no such commandment" (Acts 15:24). Without publicly stating it, the brethren in Judea had made it clear that circumcision would not be a requirement for gentile converts; however, certain principles of the law of Moses would always be in effect for Christians regardless of ethnicity.

Surprisingly, the council did not state whether Jewish converts would need to be circumcised. Perhaps any discussion of the issue was unnecessary because common cultural practice dictated that all Jews would observe this commandment, therefore making any dictum on the matter irrelevant. The decision also effectively created a physical division within the church, where those who observed all of the requirements of the Jewish law could construe their actions as somehow being part of the higher law, while those who were Gentiles were required to observe only a portion of the law and thus were living the lower law. This division would later have serious consequences for the mission to the Gentiles because the hard-line faction in Judea would continue to exert its influence in the areas where Gentiles had converted, offering a continuing reminder that they—the Gentiles—were living only a portion of the law. Paul's epistles show that the decision of the council would be a serious concern in all of the regions where he taught the gospel, ultimately forcing him to develop a consistent response to the issue of whether mankind is saved through works of the law or through grace.

ANTIOCH

The decision of the Jerusalem conference appears to have settled the waters for a short while, with Judas Barsabas and Silas returning to Jerusalem and Paul and Barnabas continuing to teach the gospel in Antioch. Shortly after the decision of the council, however, Paul decided to return to the branches where he had made contacts on his previous mission with Barnabas. He must have realized that their success on their first mission was limited by the requirement of circumcision; perhaps now that the requirement had been removed, the gospel could spread more quickly. Determined to take Barnabas with him, Paul asked, "Let us go again and visit our brethren in every city where we have preached the word of the Lord, and see how they do" (Acts 15:36).

Barnabas agreed to travel with Paul, who seems to have taken the lead for the first time, but Barnabas also desired to take his nephew John Mark with them (Acts 15:36–37). Luke records that Paul was still distressed that John Mark had left them abruptly during the first mission, probably causing them to work for their own support. Luke, who represents Paul's side in the ensuing argument, states, "Paul thought not good to take him with them, who departed from them from Pamphylia, and went not with them to the work" (Acts 15:38).

The issue over John Mark's presence on this mission may have been more profound than Luke states. According to Acts, "the contention was so sharp between them, that they departed asunder one from the other: and so Barnabas took Mark, and sailed unto Cyprus; and Paul chose Silas, and departed . . . through Syria and Cilicia" (Acts 15:39–41).

In a later letter, Paul described an event from the same time period. It may be that Acts 15 and Galatians 2 depict the same event, thus showing that when Paul recounted it to Luke he chose to focus on the issue of John Mark's departure rather than on the further schism that occurred in Antioch when Peter visited the city.

Paul's account of the event reveals that the report he later gave to Luke was much toned down and that the immediate passion of the experience had been tempered through further reflection. To fully understand the reasons for Paul's split with Barnabas, as well as the dynamics of the situation in Antioch, it is necessary to backtrack to consider more of the context of the Jerusalem conference.

According to Paul, "I went up again to Jerusalem with Barnabas, and took Titus with me also. And I went up by revelation, and communicated unto them that gospel which I preach among the Gentiles, but privately to them which were of reputation, lest by any means I should run, or had run, in vain" (Galatians 2:1–2). The sense of concern on Paul's part is immediately recognizable. His worry was that his efforts with Barnabas in Cyprus and Asia Minor would be undone because of the rigorists of the Jerusalem branch. He goes so far as saying that he was careful to communicate his report to those of "reputation," here used without any derogatory inference, so that his report would circulate from the top down rather than from the bottom up as rumor and hearsay do. To this point in the account, Paul is positive about the council and its potential outcome.

However, unknown to Paul and also to the church leaders, "false brethren" were "brought in, who came in privily to spy out our liberty" (Galatians 2:4). Time would later make explicit the association between Paul's reference to "false brethren" and Luke's "certain of the sect of the Pharisees which believed." The appearance of these false brethren was aimed at swaying the decision of the council, and Paul appears to have thought that James was either a part of the schism or had become their pawn. In his own words, which are full of sarcasm, Paul states, "To whom [the false brethren] we gave place by subjection, no, not for an hour; that the truth of the gospel might continue with you" (Galatians 2:5). Paul makes it clear that he would not accept or condone any compromise decision. This is not to say that Paul lacked confidence in the brethren, but rather that he was acutely aware of the presence of false brethren who he was afraid would have enough authority to sway the brethren. As Luke relates the story, the brethren remained in firm control.

Paul's temper and sarcasm controlled his emotions when he eventually wrote the epistle to the Galatians. Upon seeing the influence of the false brethren in Jerusalem, Paul said, "But of these who seemed to be somewhat, (whatsoever they were, it maketh no matter to me: God accepteth no man's person:) for they who seemed to be somewhat in conference added nothing to me: But contrariwise . . . they saw that the gospel of the uncircumcision was committed unto me, as the gospel of the circumcision was unto Peter" (Galatians 2:6–7). Paul is not here disparaging the leading brethren of the church, but those "who seemed to be somewhat" at the conference. He later makes it clear that these brethren should be distinguished from the pillars of the Jerusalem church, "James, Cephas, and John" (Galatians 2:9). These brethren, whether they be the Pharisaic believers in Acts or some other minority group, were bent on manipulating the decision of the council in their favor, which was to bring the Christian church back into harmony with Judaism.

Perhaps the item of greatest concern is Paul's impression of the church leadership in Jerusalem. First, he was concerned that false brethren could so easily persuade the elders and apostles into making a compromised decision, an opinion that may have resulted from his being unaware of church affairs in Jerusalem. Second, when he names the leading brethren, he refers to "James, Cephas [Peter], and John, who seemed to be pillars" (Galatians 2:9). Without doubt, the James here referred to is the Lord's brother and not James the son of Zebedee, who was called during Christ's mortal ministry. Placing the names of the brethren in this order has led some to conclude that James had been called into the Quorum of the Twelve and placed in some position similar to that of the modern First Presidency. But as

Luke's account in Acts makes clear, James acted in the role of a moderator because of his ties to the saints in Jerusalem and his family connections to Jesus. Paul, who likely was aware of such connections, felt discouraged by his presence, worrying that his efforts during his mission to the Gentiles would be rendered useless through a negative decision.

As Paul tells the story, the council decided the issue of the conversion of Gentiles favorably, a decision that was endorsed by Peter and John. Moreover, Paul relates that they asked him to make a collection for the poor saints in Jerusalem, called the Ebionim (Galatians 2:10). Paul, in his own words, records that he was anxious to help administer relief to the poor and carry the message of the council to the cities where he had made contacts with gentile families.

If the story had ended at this point, the outcome would have been entirely favorable, although a certain amount of angst would remain concerning Paul's impressions of the Jerusalem leadership. Paul relates, however, that Peter traveled to Antioch shortly after the council and there met with gentile converts. While there, "he did eat with the Gentiles: but when they [certain men who claimed to represent James] were come, he withdrew and separated himself, fearing them which were of the circumcision" (Galatians 2:12). Apparently, the men who claimed to represent James, the Lord's brother, caused Peter to feel some embarrassment over eating with Gentiles and therefore he excused himself from their presence.

James is again associated with the rigorist faction of Jerusalem, although this time James is not present but only the men who claim to represent him. The difficulty with such a situation in the early church is that these men needed only to carry a letter claiming that James had endorsed their position—a letter that could easily be forged. Moreover, James's name was becoming increasingly associated with the Jerusalem hard-liners, therefore making such a claim more credible. When viewed against the background of Acts, it is clear that James followed the leading brethren and that these new false brethren only claimed to represent his positions. Luke states that James supported the brethren and tried to offer a mediated decision that would keep the rigorists from breaking away. These men, unhappy that Peter was now favoring Gentiles, tried to make it clear that while the Jerusalem council had given them certain privileges, it had never opened the door for Jews and Gentiles to eat together, which was forbidden by Jewish belief and custom.

Their misunderstanding is now obvious, for how could the church continue to function if all Jews and Gentiles had to eat separately even though they worshipped the same God. James in his own writings, perhaps to counter the association of his name with the rigorists, encouraged Jews everywhere to focus on faith rather than asceticism and spiritual athleticism as a sign of righteousness (James 3:1–18). In Paul's defense is the simple fact that he was probably entirely unaware that James himself did not associate with these false brethren, and even though they claimed to represent him in their positions, James tried to distance himself from them. Paul was justifiably concerned.

But Peter's actions in Antioch were too much for Paul, who not only felt frustrated that these same false brethren were able to sway the actions of the president of the church, but that they were also offending those whom Paul had spent so much time trying to convert. His efforts could easily have been undermined by their insistence that Jews remain separate from Gentiles. Moreover, "Barnabas also was carried away with their dissimulation" (Galatians 2:13).

Luke records that the split with Barnabas took place over whether they should take John Mark with them, but Paul provides the reason why the argument over John Mark became so heated: Barnabas had refused to eat with Gentiles when the men who claimed to be from James came to Antioch, a decision that could have serious ramifications for their work on the second mission. When the branches learned of Barnabas's actions in Antioch, it would cast a negative light on his teachings and raise questions about his sincerity in teaching Gentiles. John Mark may have only been the ignition point for the conflagration that would catch fire between Barnabas and Paul. Fortunately the rift did not last long, as Paul later recognized the goodness of Barnabas's soul (1 Corinthians 9:6; Colossians 4:10).

The Jerusalem council represents a turbulent time in church history, and it shaped the way the church would develop thereafter. Paul and Barnabas, even though they became discouraged over certain issues associated with the conference, both realized the ramifications of the decision and immediately headed back to the cities of their previous mission to baptize those who had heard and had believed but who were not willing to undergo circumcision as a requirement for entrance into the kingdom. As Paul's own letters reveal, their missionary efforts were rewarded in a later mission as they were able to establish strong branches of the church in predominantly gentile areas.

Chapter 6

GALATIA AND BEYOND

"To be able to accept the message of Paul in those days that God really had raised the dead, for Christ had been raised from the dead and had appeared to him, was harder, possibly, to believe than the message of the prophet in this dispensation."
—*LeGrand Richards*

After spreading the news of the council's decision to the saints in Antioch, Paul and his new companion, Silas, set off towards Galatia and Asia Minor. They traveled overland, most likely making their way through Paul's hometown of Tarsus and then passing through the rugged Taurus Mountains. The trip from Antioch in Syria to Derbe, their first stopping place, would have taken the two missionaries several weeks to complete and permitted them ample opportunity for stops along the way at the homes of acquaintances. Paul may have had the opportunity to stay with his family or relatives in Tarsus.

Paul was approaching fifty years old by the time he began this mission, and the rigors of foot travel were likely taking their toll on him. Paul had previously traveled only with a small group of missionaries, but shortly after setting out on this missionary journey, Luke and possibly others joined Paul on his trip into Macedonia. Luke inserts himself into the narrative of Paul's journey quite subtly, introducing himself through a shift from telling the story in the third-person singular or plural, "he" or "they," to the first-person plural, "we." In Acts 16:10 he states, "And after he [Paul] had seen the vision, immediately we endeavoured to go into Macedonia." Up to this point in the narrative, Paul had passed through Galatia and Asia Minor and was preparing to follow a vision he had received directing him to travel into Macedonia and northern Greece. Somewhere, while passing through the areas of Paul's previous mission in Asia, his small group of missionaries was joined by Luke. Luke's purpose may have been twofold, as a missionary companion with a gentile background and also as "the beloved physician" (Colossians 4:14). Sometime during this mission, Paul's health began to decline, and the presence of Luke so early suggests that Paul was already experiencing some health-related problems in western Asia.

Also during this missionary journey, Paul found Timothy at Lystra, who "was well reported of by the brethren" (Acts 16:2). Timothy, the son of a Jewish mother and Greek father and therefore considered of Jewish descent, was circumcised according to Paul's counsel (Acts 16:1–3). The requirement of circumcision might seem strange in light of the recent decision of the Jerusalem council, but it demonstrates that two different laws were in effect, one for Jews and one for Gentiles. Rather than permit the issue of Timothy's heritage to become a stumbling block in his further missionary efforts, Paul required that he be circumcised before joining them on their travels into Macedonia. Timothy and Luke would prove themselves to be two of Paul's most trusted missionary companions.

Luke, who was probably unaware of the events that transpired in Derbe, Lystra, Pisidian Antioch, Iconium, and other cities in the region, simply passed over the entire early portion of the trip and specifically mentioned only the story of Timothy. It is not even certain from Luke's account that Paul revisited all of the cities from his previous mission to the region, which, given the fact that Luke records no baptisms during that portion, is even more surprising. If Gentiles indeed felt excluded from joining the church because they had to undergo certain obligations that had been part of the law of Moses, then the announcement of the council's decision should have opened the door to conversion. The old antagonists of the earlier mission may have, however, led those who were interested astray, possibly by pressuring them to renounce their belief in Christ or perhaps through their bad actions, which demonstrated that their newly found faith was less desirable than previously thought. Luke records only that the missionaries "were forbidden of the Holy Ghost to preach the word in Asia" (Acts 16:6).

GALATIANS

A predominant feature in most conversions is that preconversion personality traits are manifest in postconversion attitudes. For example, those who hyper-focus on their own righteousness, as Paul did, are likely to refocus themselves on the same issue after conversion with renewed vigor and understanding. Paul's preconversion zeal is readily manifest in his earliest written epistle—Galatians. Unlike the majority of his later epistles, the epistle to the Galatians is written to a region of the church rather than to the saints of a specific city. Galatia is a region in Asia Minor, the same area where Paul and Barnabas taught the gospel during an earlier mission, but where they were now forbidden to teach. Although the boundaries of the Roman province of Galatia changed dramatically after the first century, in Paul's time Galatia included the cities of Lycaonia and Pisidian Antioch, the regions around Ankara, and the plains of Pamphylia. Therefore, the epistle to the Galatians was likely written to the inhabitants of the cities Lystra, Derbe, Pisidian Antioch, and Iconium and not to some unknown community in the region of Galatia.

The recipients of the epistle are familiar with Paul, Barnabas, and Titus, all of whom were missionaries on the previous mission. Luke does not mention that Titus was present on that mission, but Paul reports that he traveled to Jerusalem to represent the gentile branches visited in that mission, thereby implying that he either traveled with them or was converted during that mission. Paul's mention of Titus in his epistle to the Galatians is almost certainly intended to be a familiar reference point, pointing their minds back to the time when Paul, Barnabas, and Titus visited them (Galatians 2:1).

For whatever reasons, Paul stayed only a short while in the territories he had visited previously. Luke records that Paul traveled into the region of Mysia, which lies along the coast of the northeastern portion of the Aegean Sea. One of the main cities of Mysia, Pergamum, had a thriving Jewish population and was later included as one of the seven churches to whom the book of Revelation was addressed. Paul chose, however, to stay away from the major population centers and traveled instead along the coast to Troas. He likely did this so he could catch a ship traveling toward the Black Sea and then head into Bithynia (Acts 16:7). By traveling back to Bithynia through the Hellespont or Straits of Dardanelle, Paul would have reentered Galatia from a more northerly route. It is clear from Luke's account that the region of Galatia was weighing heavily on the mind of Paul, who was probably perplexed that the council's decision had made very little impact in the predominantly gentile regions of Galatia. Certainly, if Paul circled back into Galatia, the saints there would have time to reconsider the full force of the Jerusalem council's decision, which should have opened the door to the gentile mission.

Paul reached the coast, where the Lord showed him a vision of a man from Macedonia. Luke hints that the vision was unexpected to Paul. Even though Galatia was still on his mind, Paul followed the inspiration he had received and traveled west into Macedonia and eventually into Greece (Acts 16:7–9), rather than east as planned. In the meantime, however, he sent off a quick letter to the saints in Galatia, a letter that reveals his frustrations, inner concerns for their welfare, and a surprising degree of his former self.

What comes to the forefront in the epistle is Paul's zeal for preaching the gospel and his wrath that his efforts have been impeded by misunderstanding and misguided presuppositions. The epistle begins without the ordinary welcome, the invocation of blessings, or the recognition of their good works. Instead, Paul turns almost immediately to his concern that someone has come to them preaching "another gospel: which is not another; but there be some that trouble you" (Galatians 1:6–7). These same antagonists were familiar with Paul; they had slandered his name among the branches in Galatia, saying that anything Paul could teach them was only derived from the teachings of other men. Initially this may seem to be a foolish concern, but it is an overt attempt to deny Paul's vision on the road to Damascus, his personal testimony, and therefore his witness of Jesus Christ (Galatians 1:11). Paul would not disagree that learning from others was necessary to spiritual progression, but his antagonists had claimed superior spiritual understanding. And in order to do so they had to discount Paul's personal experiences and claim that anything he said was only derivative, so that he had nothing substantial to offer those he taught.

The account that follows of Paul's vision on the road to Damascus, his trip to Jerusalem to report on the success of the gentile mission, and Peter's trip to Antioch are all given in the context of Paul defending his personal testimony of Jesus Christ and his claim to have had a personal vision of the resurrected Savior. Following the definition of an apostle set forth in Acts 1, which states that an apostle needed to be a personal witness of the Resurrection, Paul tells the saints in Galatia that he was made "an apostle, (not of men, neither by man [Peter], but by Jesus Christ, and God the Father, who raised him from the dead)" (Galatians 1:1). Paul, whose calling as an apostle has been the subject of great debate, used the definition of an apostle set forth in Acts and therefore openly proclaimed his apostleship, while making sure to differentiate that at this stage he was not called into the quorum (i.e., not called by a man). In context, Paul was testifying that his opponents were wrong to claim that his testimony was only derivative.

Paul's former personality comes to light in Galatians when he relates for the first time "how that beyond measure I persecuted the church of God, and wasted it: and profited in the Jews' religion above many my equals in mine own nation, being more exceedingly zealous of the traditions of my fathers" (Galatians 1:13–14). Paul also reminds his Jewish antagonists that during his vision on the road to Damascus that God called him "that I might preach him among the heathen" (Galatians 1:16). Paul then moves to connect the "false brethren" of the Jerusalem conference, who tried to alter Christianity according to their own Jewish sympathies, with the false brethren who had such great influence in Galatia, who also tried to circumvent Paul's missionary activity by imposing their own brand of Jewish Christianity upon the saints (Galatians 2:4).

In Paul's denunciation of Peter for his actions in Antioch and of the men from James who caused Peter and Barnabas to offend Gentiles in the city, there is a sense of zealous exuberance that was not subject to restraint (Galatians 2:11–13). Paul's frustration was compounded by the facts that Galatia had effectively been closed to further missionary work and that ultimately Jewish sympathizers were able to corrupt the branches there. To show that these false brethren in Galatia should receive the greater condemnation, Paul responded by telling the members that even Peter was incorrect to not eat with Gentiles. To counter the inroads made by these Jewish sympathizers, Paul initiated a discussion that he would more fully develop later—how salvation depends upon grace and works, although it relies more heavily on grace. Paul's thoughts on the subject appear in their infancy in Galatians, while by the time that he wrote Romans he had thought through the subject more carefully.

Paul's Thoughts on His Own Salvation

One of the surprising aspects of Paul's teachings was his consistent recommendation for the saints to be "as I am," a recommendation that borders on pride. A recommendation to be like Jesus or to follow the prophet are acceptable and common directives, but encouragement to be like one of the many Christian missionaries is surprising. Implied in Paul's statement is his preconversion attitude that "touching the righteousness which is in the law, [I was] blameless" (Philippians 3:6). Paul felt that he was blameless as a Jew, a sentiment that generated a significant amount of confidence, perhaps overconfidence, in his own standing before the Lord. When Paul converted to Christianity, those feelings of blamelessness transferred into feelings of righteousness, which in turn led him to put himself forward as an example worthy of emulation. He wrote to the Corinthians at the beginning of a later missionary journey to "be ye followers of me" (1 Corinthians 4:16). Only later did Paul qualify this remark by saying, "Be ye followers of me, even as I also am of Christ" (1 Corinthians 11:1). The qualifier "as I also am of Christ" is not found in his earlier statements, suggesting that Paul's personality was getting in the way of the gospel of Jesus Christ.

Another powerful insight into Paul's character comes from his denunciation of Peter. Paul, a student of the Old Testament, should have been aware of the precedent set forth when David had regard for Saul, the Lord's anointed. When David found Saul, his enemy, sleeping in a cave he refused to harm him, instead teaching, "I will not put forth mine hand against my lord; for he is the Lord's anointed" (1 Samuel 24:10). Paul, on the other hand, openly rebuked the president of the church. Even if Peter were to blame for his actions in Antioch, Paul should have used some restraint as David did before him. Joseph Smith taught, "It is an eternal principle, that has existed with God from all eternity: That man who rises up to condemn others, finding fault with the Church, saying that they are out of the way, while he himself is righteous, then know assuredly, that that man is in the high road to apostasy; and if he does not repent, will apostatize, as God lives" (*Teachings of the Prophet Joseph Smith,* 156–57). Paul, who could have exercised restraint in relating Peter's actions, placed himself in a position where the only person whom he could confidently recommend was himself.

Paul's Thorn in the Flesh

Fortunately, the Lord in his infinite wisdom can foresee and help curtail such spiritual excess. At the same time that Paul wrote to the saints in Galatia, he began also speaking of a thorn in the flesh, a physical malady that plagued him throughout the remainder of his missionary travels. He thanked the saints for not despising his malady, which must have been readily visible, saying, "Ye know how through infirmity of the flesh I preached the gospel unto you at the first. And my temptation which was in my flesh ye despised not, nor rejected" (Galatians 4:13–14). Although these passages provide no indication of the nature of Paul's physical ailment, a further verse specifies its nature: "If it had been possible, ye would have plucked out your own eyes, and have given them to me," a statement that only makes sense if Paul needed their eyes because his were damaged (Galatians 4:15). A later account by Luke implies the same nature for Paul's sickness: "Then said Paul unto him, God shall smite thee, thou whited wall: for sittest thou to judge me after the law, and commandest me to be smitten contrary to the law? And they that stood by said, Revilest thou God's high priest? Then said Paul, I wist not, brethren, that he was the high priest" (Acts 23:3–5). Luke's account makes sense if Paul could not see it was the high priest speaking to him, a person to whom he would otherwise have shown greater respect. At the end of Galatians Paul writes, "Ye see how large a letter I have written unto you with mine own hand" (Galatians 6:11), an indication that he couldn't see well enough to write in smaller print. Paul used his large handwriting as a sign that he personally wrote the epistle.

The importance of this thorn in the flesh was not realized until much later. Paul begins to mention the thorn in the flesh at a time when an old missionary field was stagnating and enemies within the church were thwarting his new attempts. Moreover, Paul felt that Peter's actions in Antioch had a direct impact on his ability to teach the gospel in Galatia. He returned to his preconversion attitude of perfection and superiority, and recommended that his example was worthy of emulation. At this same time, Luke the physician became a fellow missionary with Paul, suggesting that the thorn in the flesh was an actual physical ailment. All of these facts, when taken together, demonstrate that Paul was given the thorn in the flesh to remind him to be humble and rely on the Lord and look to the proper priesthood authorities. Paul, like anyone who is ill, sought the help of a trusted physician, only to realize that Luke could not heal him.

Much later in his life Paul revealed to the Corinthian saints, "Lest I should be exalted above measure through the abundance of the revelations, there was given to me a thorn in the flesh, the messenger of Satan to buffet me, lest I should be exalted above measure. For this thing I besought the Lord thrice, that it might depart from me. And he said unto me, My grace is sufficient for thee: for my strength is made perfect in weakness" (2 Corinthians 12:7–9). At first Paul sought the care of a physician, who could not help, so Paul sought the Lord, who intentionally left the ailment intact. Paul relates that it was given to him to remind him that an abundance of revelations did not guarantee his righteousness and standing before the Lord. In Galatians, the theme of humility is reinforced by Paul's thorn in the flesh, which was a constant reminder to him to continually rely on the power of the Lord.

Justified by Faith in Christ

There is a human tendency to advertise, sometimes subtly, personal righteousness at the same time as seeking justification. Internally, justification satisfies the human desire for recognition, but until that divine acknowledgment is extended, drawing attention to good works is a necessary part of the human progression towards perfection. No one can go quietly to salvation as the last vestiges of pride are stripped away, exposing a bare soul, which needs to cover itself with good works and actions.

Paul did not come away from the road-to-Damascus experience a saved man. That only redirected his passions and his energy into more favorable pursuits. Justification, or perfection according to law, stands as a stepping-stone to sanctification, which in turn means being made holy through the grace of God. Galatians shows that justification was a subject of great concern to Paul, as well as a telling sign of the status of his own spiritual progression. For an individual steeped in the works of the law, conversion to Christianity must have been liberating but at the same time frustrating because he no longer lived the law of

Moses with its extensive set of physical, externally indentifiable, commandments.

In the Old Testament, Paul found a scriptural precedent for the differences between Judaism and Christianity. He taught, "Cursed is every one that continueth not in all things which are written in the book of the law to do them. But that no man is justified by the law in the sight of God, it is evident: for, The just shall live by faith" (Galatians 3:10–11; see also Deuteronomy 27:26; Habakkuk 2:4). The Old Testament contains evidence for two complementary paths to salvation—through the works of the law (Paul's ancestral religion) and through faith (Christianity). Paul argued to the saints in Galatia that the latter is superior to the former, that works of the law become a standard which all men fall short of, while faith in Jesus Christ leads to justification (Galatians 2:16). Perhaps the most succinct statement in scripture on the relationship of the two paths comes from Galatians where Paul says, "the law was our schoolmaster to bring us unto Christ, that we might be justified by faith. But after that faith is come, we are no longer under a schoolmaster" (Galatians 3:24–25). One law prepared the ground while the other law brought with it the fulness, but both were equally essential to salvation.

The law of faith, as Paul calls it, demands that the doers "live in the Spirit" and "walk in the Spirit" and that they "bear . . . one another's burdens, and so fulfill the law of Christ" (Galatians 5:25; 6:2). Paul never advocated salvation by doing nothing, but rather argued that with Christ there had been a shift in requirements. The works of the law of his youth, or in other words the law of Moses, "profit you nothing," while the works of the law of Christ lead to hope and salvation (Galatians 5:1–7). Paul, who advocated, perhaps more than any other New Testament author, that salvation was administered by grace, worked with all his might. He was tireless in the cause of

Christianity, spending his entire adult life in missionary service. If salvation were given as a free gift, then Paul's unrelenting pursuit of justification makes little sense.

SAMOTHRACE, NEAPOLIS, PHILIPPI

Shortly after writing to the saints in Galatia, Paul set out by boat to travel into Macedonia, stopping at the port cities of Samothrace, probably to unload cargo and then at the port of Neapolis (modern Kavalla), about ten miles from the city center of Philippi. The two cities are connected by the famous Egnatian Way, a major Roman road between the Aegean and Adriatic Seas. As Paul and his missionary companions disembarked they also set foot in Europe for the first time. Even though Paul passed through several smaller cities where he could have preached the gospel, it appears that he made his way immediately to Philippi, a Roman colony with a small Jewish population.

This Roman road connected the Aegean Sea to the Adriatic Sea. After arriving in the port city of Neapolis, Paul and his missionary companions traveled this road to Philippi.

The Roman colony of Philippi was impressive, boasting a large forum and a noteworthy theater in later centuries. In Paul's day, the city benefited from its strategic placement along the largest Roman road in the region, which although in need of repair still attracted significant commerce. Philippi also benefited from its port city of Neapolis, where goods shipped in from the East began transport to various inland cities. The abundance of imported marble suggests that Philippi became the hub of commercial activity in the region.

Roman soldiers who had fought under Marc Antony and Augustus at the battle of Actium (30 B.C.), and their descendants, inhabited the colony. Typically such soldiers would be granted land in Italy, but as land in their home country became more of a luxury, soldiers were given land grants in eastern colonies on the frontiers of the Roman empire. The soldiers would have interacted with a smaller Thracian population indigenous to the region, who spoke a foreign tongue, as well as the older Greek inhabitants. The shrines and temples that can be definitively dated to the time of Paul attest to the city's cosmopolitan environment. Shrines to local heroes, the Olympian gods, Dionysus, the Samothracian Great gods, and a host of other deities could be found within the city. The largest structures and sanctuaries were to deceased heroes, attesting to the soldiers' fascination and reverence for military glory. In addition to soldiers, the colony would also have housed a large slave population to work the estates given to the colonists, slaves who had been taken as spoils of war.

The Jewish population in Philippi is more difficult to account for. The large number of inscriptions in Latin and Greek suggest that any Jewish population in the city had been assimilated into the larger culture. If there was a Jewish synagogue or burial ground in the region, then it has yet to be discovered. A Jewish burial inscription has been found near the necropolis of the city, but it can only be dated to the second century. That the city had only a small Jewish population seems to be confirmed by Luke's account of what transpired there.

As was his custom in other major population centers, Paul sought out the local Jewish congregation, but instead of finding a large synagogue, he found a place "by a river side, where prayer was wont to be made" (Acts 16:13). He found a small number of women there, of whom Lydia is specified, but no men are mentioned. This suggests not an official synagogue but rather a gathering place for a small population of Jews, some of whom were probably slaves who served the predominantly Roman citizenry.

The absence of any males at their worship services is surprising, but may be a testimony to the small number of Jews in the city. Lydia is said to have come from Thyatira and to have "worshipped God," indicating she was not Jewish but had converted to Judaism (Acts 16:14). Her presence as one of the few gathered to worship God reveals her devoted heart. Upon hearing Paul and Silas teach, Lydia was baptized with all of her household. Immediately after her conversion, she "besought us, saying, If ye have judged me to be faithful to the Lord, come into my house, and abide there. And she constrained us" (Acts 16:15). Lydia thus became the first known European convert to the church and the first convert mentioned by name during the second mission. Unfortunately, Paul is silent about his actions during this period of the second mission. It appears that he stayed in Philippi for some time, remaining hopeful that his success with Lydia and her family would translate into other successes.

Paul's First Imprisonment—Philippi

Philippi proved more challenging than Paul and Silas had anticipated, as both of them were beaten and jailed for healing a soothsayer or sorcerer. A slave girl had previously prophesied that "these men are the servants of the most high God, which shew unto us the way of salvation" (Acts 16:17). Her prophecy is hardly prophetic, revealing only her knowledge that they were missionaries who represented the "most high God," a typically Jewish description of the Father. Her description of their work fits either a Jewish or Christian missionary quite well, and according to Luke's account her constant "prophecies" became annoying (Acts 16:18). In order to put an end to her harangue, Paul healed her.

The healing resulted in Paul and Silas's imprisonment because the sorceress's master had now lost a substantial amount of income. He complained of Paul's actions to the local magistrates, as either a loss of or damage to personal property or for introducing foreign religious practices that were damaging to civic well-being (Acts 16:21). Paul and Silas, in the process of the hearing, were disparaged as "Jews," which in this

The entrance to the prison where Paul and Silas were likely held overnight in Philippi. The prison is located near the theater and may have been used as a cistern prior to being converted into a prison. No other prison has been identified at Philippi, making this structure the most probable place where they were held.

The interior of the prison in Philippi. The roof is supported with wood beams, but in Paul's day the walls and ceiling were likely stuccoed. The small room had no windows or ventilation shafts, and therefore the only source of sunlight and air would be through the entrance.

context is used as a term of derision (Acts 16:20). Without any official trial, Paul and Silas were beaten at the command of the local magistrates and then locked away in prison. The actions of the local magistrates suggest they thought of the missionaries as wandering riffraff who would leave the city with a little coercion.

Unfortunately for the local magistrates, Paul and Silas were both Roman citizens (Acts 16:37). Therefore, the law guaranteed them certain protections, one of which was the ability to confront any accusers in a court that held legal jurisdiction over the accused. The court had to hear the accused as well as the accusers prior to any sentence being meted out.

The modern prison system provides an inaccurate point of comparison to its ancient counterpart. In the modern system, prisoners are incarcerated for significant amounts of time in the hope they can reflect on their actions and reform their behavior.

Prisoners have rights, and certain conditions must be met so that their incarceration is just and fair. The Roman prison system harbored no such illusions, and only occasionally was an individual placed in a prison for any significant amount of time. Those whose dignity and status warranted special treatment were banished to distant lands or islands so that their influence could be isolated and controlled, while lesser criminals were held in prison while they awaited execution, usually for only a few weeks. The time between Jesus' arrest and crucifixion is not remarkably short by ancient standards. For the most part, the prison system of the Roman Empire was a ruthless institution, striking fear and dread in the hearts of those who faced imprisonment. It is not uncommon to read accounts of those in the ancient world who committed suicide rather than face incarceration.

One account of being imprisoned records, "Consequently, he sickened at length and was ill, as might be expected in view of the fact that he slept on the ground and at night could not even stretch out his legs, which were confined in the stocks. By day, to be sure, the collar was sufficient, together with manacles upon one hand; but for the night he had to be fully secured by his bonds. Moreover, the stench of the room and its stifling air (since many were confined in the same place, cramped for room, and scarcely able to draw breath), the clash of iron, the scanty sleep—all these conditions were difficult and intolerable for such a man, unwonted to them and unschooled to a life so rigorous" (Lucian, *Toxaris,* 29). Living conditions were intolerable because those in prison were not expected to live very long. The terrible conditions of Roman prisons led to the death of many prior to their formal executions. Philostratus's account of imprisonment relates, "Some of them were ill, others were despondent and resigned, others faced death boldly, others groaned for their children, parents, and marriages" (*The Life of*

Apollonius of Tyana, 7.26). Luke records similarly, "And at midnight Paul and Silas prayed, and sang praises unto God: and the prisoners heard them" (Acts 16:25). What Luke recorded as a positive experience was almost certainly understood as a sign of despair by those around them.

Luke records that the imprisonment of Paul and Silas was for only a single night. However, Luke also appears to have departed Paul's company prior to their arrest and imprisonment. He was aware of the prophecies of the sorceress in Philippi, but when detailing the events of the arrest, he included only Paul and Silas. Luke did not personally reinsert himself in the story until halfway through Paul's last missionary journey when he, along with several other missionaries, waited to meet Paul at Troas (Acts 16:17; 20:5). Therefore, his compression of the events at Philippi may represent only the outline of the story. In his next epistle (1 Thessalonians), Paul exhibits a tenderness that is not present in his epistle to the Galatians, revealing that the imprisonment may have worn some of his rough edges smooth.

Paul and Silas Are Delivered from Prison

Unfortunately, Luke's narrative lacks the necessary detail that would clarify the nature of their imprisonment. The traditional site of the prison is near the center of town, very near the amphitheater, suggesting it was used as a temporary holding cell for criminals awaiting execution. Luke records that other prisoners were with Paul and Silas in the cell, which is large enough for about four to six people to lie on the ground comfortably but without any separate rest room facility. It was likely used at one time as a cistern for water storage, but perhaps due to a crack in the structure it was later converted into a temporary holding cell. The prisoners may have been lowered down into the cell by a rope or makeshift ladder.

Prisoners were usually given meager rations, just enough to

keep them alive but not enough to make them comfortable. Family members were often permitted to bring food or clothing to the condemned, but food and other luxury items often became the immediate property of the entire prison population. Political prisoners were an especially difficult case because guards and keepers would be required to take note of anyone who spoke with or visited the condemned, thereby implicating them in the same crimes. There were no rules protecting the human rights of the imprisoned, particularly in the provinces and colonies away from the nexus of the capital city. Prisoners were often flogged, tortured, and starved to force them into revealing information or confessing to their crimes. The actual cell, with all its filth and sickness, became a temporary place for the broken and wounded to convalesce. Paul and Silas, like many other criminals, were beaten prior to being imprisoned (Acts 16:23). Luke was not aware how severely they were wounded, but does mention that they left town immediately after their release, indicating they were healthy enough to travel but wary of staying in the city.

During the first night of their imprisonment, sometime near midnight, an earthquake damaged the prison so those who were incarcerated were able to escape. Luke states that "the foundations of the prison were shaken," suggesting that perhaps the building partially collapsed (Acts 16:26).

Something that took place during Paul and Silas's miraculous release appears to have led the jailer to assume that they had somehow exercised power to cause the earthquake and loose the bands of all the prisoners. He immediately approached the two missionaries and asked, "Sirs, what must I do to be saved?" (Acts 16:30). Furthermore, the jailer brought the two missionaries to his house and fed them, which led to his conversion and that of his household. After leaving the house of the jailer, Paul and Silas stopped briefly at the home of Lydia to confirm to her and those who were worried about their safety that they were well. They immediately left the city and headed east toward Thessalonica.

AMPHIPOLIS, APOLLONIA, AND THESSALONICA

Paul and Silas traveled overland to Thessalonica, stopping briefly in the small villages of Amphipolis and Apollonia, which were easily accessible along the Egnatian Way. The risk of theft along such rural roads was significant, and certain precautions, such as traveling in groups, had to be taken in order to maintain safety. Traveling between Philippi and Thessalonica would have taken the missionary group about ten days. The first part of their journey, from the mountainous region around Philippi to Amphipolis on the coast, would have been the most difficult. Foot travel would have been much easier, perhaps quite enjoyable, from Amphipolis to Apollonia, with pleasant scenery and a relatively flat road. Although later tradition claims that Paul and Silas worked in these two communities along the way, Luke seems to indicate that they stopped there only for rest and nourishment. Thessalonica, the major urban center of the region, was their ultimate destination, and like other population centers along the Aegean Sea coast, it had a healthy and thriving Jewish community.

Almost every synagogue outside of Jerusalem attracted large numbers of sympathizers or interested observers, who felt some attraction toward Judaism or even believed in some of its tenets but were unwilling to take on all the responsibilities of becoming a member in full fellowship. When Christianity was first taught in these synagogues, these sympathizers flocked to the new religious movement, which did not obligate them to observe the same physical requirements that Judaism did. The conversion of these sympathizers, who are often referred to as "God-fearers" or "proselytes" in the New Testament, led to friction between the local Jewish communities who lost some of their members to the traveling Christian missionaries. Even though these sympathizers may not have been numbered among the members in full fellowship of the local Jewish synagogue, they were counted as friends, and the hope was that they would ultimately take the steps toward conversion.

As was Paul's practice, he "went in unto them [in the synagogue], and three sabbath days reasoned with them out of the scriptures" (Acts 17:2). This practice had a profound effect among the Jews of the synagogue as well as the sympathizers, who, "of the devout Greeks a great multitude, and of the chief women not a few," believed (Acts 17:4). Luke records that their interest in Paul's message touched off a near-riot in Thessalonica and that one convert—Jason—was hauled before the magistrates and accused of sedition. According to Luke's account, Paul and Silas's missionary activity in the city was short-lived, and the two were run out of the city after only a few weeks.

Paul's account of the same time period differs slightly in that he came away concerned and hopeful for the newly founded branch in the city. After leaving the city of Thessalonica at night, Paul, Silas, and Timothy headed south through Berea toward Athens, no doubt hoping to find an untouched field ready to harvest. Athens was the largest city in the region and was considered by many to be the cultural center of the Mediterranean region. Only Rome was a rival to Athens in matters of culture and education, and perhaps Paul felt that its citizens would be more open-minded to their message than the Jews of Thessalonica.

After traveling the short distance to Berea, Paul and Silas began teaching the gospel to the local congregation of Jews, who appear to have accepted them warmly. Despite their initial success in Berea, when "the Jews of Thessalonica had knowledge that the word of God was preached of Paul at Berea, they came thither also, and stirred up the people" (Acts 17:13). Although not directly aligned or in contact with the rigorists in Judea, the congregation of Jews in Thessalonica were apparently afraid that allowing certain exceptions for Gentiles to enter the church might lead to disaffection among Jewish members, or perhaps might lead to them becoming lax in their obedience to the law. Paul's success in these regions was among the Greeks who came to the synagogue to hear the word, but not among those who were Jewish by birth (Acts 17:4, 12).

Had Paul and Silas come to Thessalonica and taught the gospel to those who had had no contacts with the local Jewish congregation, there would have been no uproar among the Jews. For Paul and Silas the synagogue represented the crossroads of Judaism and Christianity, a place where the old and new met. For the local Jews, the synagogue was the place where two heretical Diaspora missionaries came to lead a part of their congregation astray, teaching that they did not need to live the whole law to be saved. The local leaders appear to have been afraid Christianity would lower the requirements for salvation, which would cause many members to flock to these new teachings. Their fear inspired deep-seated prejudices, which in turn took command of their otherwise docile temperaments, ultimately leading them to expunge what was new and true.

Paul does not provide any detailed report for the events that transpired in Thessalonica and Berea, although Luke's account leaves the impression that Paul's life was in danger. Sensing that the Jews of Thessalonica had pursued him to Berea, and that they intended to do him harm, "the brethren sent away Paul to go as it were to the sea: but Silas and Timotheus abode there still" (Acts 17:14). Luke does not record how Paul then traveled to Athens, but only that the brethren of Berea took him "to the sea," "as far as the sea," or as some manuscripts report, "as though he would travel by sea." The trip to the sea, in Luke's mind, was a ruse to divert Paul's opponents who specifically sought his life.

Paul's opponents, who arrived in Berea to find only his fellow missionaries, must have become confused at the reports that Paul had left the city and headed toward the sea. Because Paul was able to arrive in Athens much sooner than those whom he had left behind in Berea, it is likely that he did ultimately travel by sea, it being much quicker than taking the land route. While he waited in Athens for his missionary companions to arrive, Paul began to teach the gospel there. For reasons now unknown, the threat to Silas and Timothy was not significant; therefore, they were able to remain behind in Berea to act as decoys.

After a short while (Luke was unaware how long), Silas and Timothy arrived in Athens to find Paul teaching the gospel to the citizens there. When Timothy reported how the crisis in Berea was resolved, Paul became anxious about the saints of Thessalonica. Paul said, in his own words, "Wherefore when we could no longer forbear, we thought it good to be left at Athens alone; and sent Timotheus . . . to comfort you concerning your faith" (1 Thessalonians 3:1–2). From Paul's statements, it appears that either Timothy was not under any threat in Thessalonica or that he would travel back to the city secretly and find out what he could.

While Timothy was traveling back to Thessalonica to inquire of the saints there, Luke introduces some details of Paul's success in Athens. Luke felt that the events in Athens were important enough to report, while Paul never mentioned what took place there, perhaps because of worry about the fledgling branch in Thessalonica.

Paul did not write 1 Thessalonians until after Timothy had reported back to him about matters there. Luke reports that

Overlooking the modern city of Athens, Mars Hill was the location of Paul's famous speech to the Athenians. Dionysius the Areopagite and Damaris heard Paul speak from this hill and accepted the gospel (Acts 17:22–34).

Silas also traveled with Timothy to Thessalonica, thus leaving Paul alone in Athens and Corinth. Timothy, who found Paul in Corinth, which lies about sixty miles west of Athens, brought with him a positive report of the small congregation of saints they had left behind in Thessalonica, although Luke, who had departed from the group previously, reports that Timothy's report caused Paul to be "pressed in the spirit" (Acts 18:5). Certainly there is a negative aspect of 1 Thessalonians, written after Paul had received information about the branch there, but his anger and concern were over the rigorist faction in the city and not over the faith of the saints themselves. Luke does not differentiate between concern for the saints and concern for their persecutions. Paul, who probably gave Luke the impression that he was distressed over the situation in Thessalonica, appears to have rejoiced at hearing how the saints had remained faithful. Timothy's report apparently satisfied Paul, who continued his missionary work in Corinth and began gathering his thoughts prior to writing a letter to the saints in Thessalonica.

Paul's Account of His Stay in Thessalonica

In writing to the saints in Thessalonica, Paul records that they had "received the word in much affliction, with joy of the Holy Ghost: So that ye were ensamples to all that believe in Macedonia and Achaia. For from you sounded out the word of the Lord not only in Macedonia and Achaia, but also in every place your faith to God-ward is spread abroad; so that we need not to speak any thing" (1 Thessalonians 1:6–8). Although Luke gives the impression that Paul, Silas, and Timothy were run out of town before they could accomplish anything significant in Thessalonica, Paul lauds the saints for having converted to the gospel amidst affliction and for becoming an example to their brethren in Macedonia and Greece (Achaia). Luke was not aware why the Jews of Thessalonica were so aggressive in their pursuit of Paul, but Paul's account provides the missing information. Their conversion was exemplary, perhaps because of the number who converted or because of how the saints there overcame significant adversity to accept the gospel message. Paul also confirms that those who converted were not Jews, but rather Greek-speaking Gentiles (1 Thessalonians 2:14–16; 4:1–5). When news of their conversion spread throughout the region, the local Jewish leaders feared that the details might convince other Jewish sympathizers to become disaffected or, even worse, might influence some Jews to convert to the Christian message.

The Philippian imprisonment was a direct result of Paul and Silas's use of the priesthood, but the events in Thessalonica would kindle the fires of opposition that would continually impede Paul's later missionary activities. A more organized resistance developed to the spread of Christianity within Jewish congregations in the Mediterranean regions, and a series of anti-Christian missions by rigorist Jews sought to set matters straight.

Some specific details about Paul's stay in Thessalonica emerge from his first letter to converts there. While Luke can only confirm that Paul was in the city for at least three weeks, Paul writes of their "labour and travail: for labouring night and day, because we would not be chargeable unto any of you, we preached unto you the gospel of God" (1 Thessalonians 2:9). This reference is not intended only as a gentle reminder of Paul's diligence in teaching the gospel message among them; it is also meant to subtly compare those who afflicted the saints and persecuted Paul with Paul himself, who worked to support himself and did not ask money from the members to help him during his stay. The missionaries were not a financial burden for the local saints, and Paul reminded them that he and his companions worked "night and day" to support themselves while they were in Thessalonica so that they could bring them the gospel; a demonstration not only of their diligence but also of their sincerity.

Paul's letter also seems to confirm Luke's report that the missionaries had been run out of town. In Paul's words: "But we, brethren, being taken from you for a short time in presence, not in heart, endeavoured the more abundantly to see your face with great desire. Wherefore we would have come unto you, even I Paul, once and again; but Satan hindered us" (1 Thessalonians 2:17–18). This passage seems to imply that the brethren, after leaving the city, hoped to return immediately. Luke reports that the missionaries went to Berea, and that the brethren then headed south toward Athens, but Paul makes it clear that the branch in Thessalonica was on his mind immediately after his departure and that he had hoped to come back to them but could not because of local opposition. Athens then became a second choice for the missionaries, who designated it as a location where they could regroup. Because Paul could not travel back to Thessalonica himself, he sent Timothy and Silas to find out what had transpired after their departure. Why Paul was forbidden from returning while the other missionaries were not is unclear. Paul's mediocre reception in Athens, and the departure of Timothy and Silas, pushed him to search out a new missionary frontier—Corinth.

PAUL'S STAY IN CORINTH

Shortly after his own arrival in Corinth, Paul was joined by Timothy and Silas, who reported events that had transpired in Macedonia since Paul's departure. Paul absorbed the implications of their report and turned his attention to the potentially rich field ahead of him. With a thriving Jewish community living alongside Greeks and Romans, Corinth offered the ideal location to preach the gospel to the whole world. Without the intellectual trappings and presumptuousness of Athens, Corinth was a microcosm of the Roman empire, where Rome ruled Greek subjects who tolerated the Jews who lived and worked among them.

Corinth had both a colorful and rich history. The name of the city is derived from a Greek word meaning *to fornicate*, a less than subtle reference to the type of merchandise commonly available for those who made their homes there. Legendary not only for her promiscuous culture, Corinth also boasted a thriving economy in the first century under Roman expansion and rule. The city controlled two major harbors, one to the east (Cenchrea) in the Saronic Gulf and the other in the Gulf of Corinth. The Isthmus of Corinth was a major thoroughfare for merchant vessels, which could be unloaded and their merchandise carried overland to the other port more quickly than it could be transported by sailing around Sparta and on to Italy. The rulers of Corinth controlled shipping and transport across the Isthmus, thereby providing the city with significant tax revenue and business for those who transported the ships' cargo.

One ancient visitor reported: "Corinth is called 'wealthy' because of its commerce, since it is situated on the Isthmus and is master of two harbours, of which the one leads straight to Asia, and the other to Italy; and it makes easy the exchange of merchandise from both countries that are so far distant from each other. . . . But to the Corinthians of later times still greater advantages were added, for also the Isthmian Games, which were celebrated there, were wont to draw crowds of people. And the Bacchiadae, a rich and numerous and illustrious family, became tyrants of Corinth, and held their empire for nearly two hundred years, and without disturbance reaped the fruits of the commerce; and when Cypselus overthrew these, he himself became tyrant, and his house endured for three generations; and an evidence of the wealth of this house is the offering which Cypselus dedicated at Olympia, a huge statue of beaten gold. Again, Demaratus, one of the men who had been in power at Corinth, fleeing from the seditions there, carried with him so much wealth from his home to Tyrrhenia that not only he himself became the ruler of the city that admitted him, but his son was made king of the Romans. And the temple of Aphrodite was so rich that it owned more than a thousand temple-slaves, courtesans, whom both men and women had dedicated to the goddess. And therefore it was also on account of these women that the city was crowded with people and grew rich; for instance, the ship-captains freely squandered their money, and hence the proverb, 'Not for every man is the voyage to Corinth'" (Strabo, *Geography*, 8.6.20).

The peculiar attitude of the Corinthians is well demonstrated in a story about them that was still being retold hundreds of years after it occurred. Strabo reports the story thus: "The Corinthians, when they were subject to Philip, not only sided with him in his quarrel with the Romans, but individually behaved so contemptuously towards the Romans that certain persons ventured to pour down filth upon the Roman ambassadors when passing by their house" (*Geography*, 8.6.23). Even though they were subjected to Roman rule, the citizens of Corinth maintained a firm hold on their own individuality.

Paul may have sought out Corinth for its sea air and its healthy environment. Although he does not specifically mention his health in the letter that he composed during his stay in Corinth, his earlier letter had specifically mentioned he was suffering from some type of ailment. After leaving Berea, Paul stayed in two coastal cities—Athens and Corinth—perhaps in an effort to improve his health under conditions similar to his hometown of Tarsus.

After arriving in Corinth, Paul met "a certain Jew named Aquila, born in Pontus, lately come from Italy, with his wife Priscilla; (because that Claudius had commanded all Jews to depart from Rome:) and came unto them. And because he was of the same craft, he abode with them, and wrought: for by their occupation they were tentmakers" (Acts 18:2–3). Accounts differ in explaining why the Jews were ultimately expelled from Rome under the emperor Claudius (A.D. 41–54). Josephus records: "There was a man who was a Jew, but had been driven away from his own country by an accusation laid against him for transgressing their laws, and by the fear he was under of punishment for the same; but in all respects a wicked man:—he then living at Rome, professed to instruct men in the wisdom of the laws of Moses. He procured also three other men, entirely of the same character with himself, to be his partners. These men persuaded Fulvia, a woman of great dignity, and one that had embraced the Jewish religion, to send purple and gold to the temple at Jerusalem; and, when they had gotten them, they employed them for their own uses, and spent the money themselves; on which account it was that they at first required it of her. Whereupon Tiberius, who had been informed of the thing by Saturninus, the husband of Fulvia, who desired inquiry might be made about it, ordered all the Jews to be banished out of Rome; at which time the consuls listed four thousand men out of them, and sent them to the island Sardinia; but punished a greater number of them, who were unwilling to become soldiers on account of keeping the laws of their forefathers. Thus were these Jews banished out of the city by the wickedness of four men" (*Antiquities*, 18.3.5).

Another historian blamed the expulsion of the Jews on their constant "disturbances at the instigation of Chrestus [a misspelling of Christ]." Because of those disturbances, Claudius "expelled them from Rome" (Suetonius, *The Lives of the Caesars*, 5.25). Historically, the reason that the Jews were expelled from Rome is likely a result of disturbances among Jews concerning whether Jesus was the Christ. The expulsion of the entire population of Jews from the capital because of the wickedness of four men seems unlikely and out of character for the emperor Claudius or for Tiberius. On the other hand, as Christian missionaries arrived in Rome around A.D. 50, there were likely to be disturbances between those who believed and those who felt that Christianity was a perversion of Jewish law and practice. Other cities had seen similar revolts, and Claudius, rather than settle the dispute, cast all of them out. The "Jew" Aquila may therefore have been a believing Christian who together with all others of Jewish heritage was sent away during the expulsion by Claudius.

Fortuitously, Paul quickly made contacts with those who had already heard of Christ. Even if they were not believers, they would have had some understanding of the debates going on in Rome and the reasons for their expulsion from their homes. As is so often the case, one missionary prepared them, while another missionary (Paul) was put in a position to reap the seeds that had been sown. Peter was almost certainly the first apostle to teach the gospel in Rome, and the conversion of Aquila and Priscilla in Corinth may have been a direct result of their hearing the gospel from Peter and his fellow companions there.

Paul's stay in Corinth, unlike his ministry in Galatia and Macedonia, endured for a considerable amount of time. At the conclusion of his stay there, which lasted eighteen months, Paul departed peacefully (Acts 18:11, 18). Even though he faced some opposition from members of the local synagogue, the missionaries were able to establish a strong branch in the city, one that was not under any immediate threat of persecution.

Paul's stay in Corinth can also be dated with exactness. While he was there, he was brought before, "Gallio . . . the deputy of Achaia" (Acts 18:12). Gallio, or more properly L. Iunius Gallio Annaeanus, was proconsul of Greece (Achaia) from May 1, 51, through April 30, 52, indicating that Paul, who

These storefronts line the main road going into the city of Corinth. Paul worked with Priscilla and Aquila in a small shop similar to these in Corinth.

was in Corinth during the governorship of Gallio, must have been there for at least a portion of that year. Luke seems to indicate that Paul was in the city prior to Gallio's arrival there and that Paul stayed even after Gallio had returned to Rome, which when taken together would indicate that Paul was in Corinth from late winter of A.D. 50 to the summer of A.D. 51. Nearly all other dates from Paul's ministry are calculated using his stay in Corinth as a fixed point.

Luke notes two events that transpired in Corinth. First, he records that Paul had become frustrated because his work among the Jews of the local synagogue was progressing slowly and because the congregation there had rejected the teaching that Jesus was the Messiah. As had happened earlier, Paul's temper took control of his emotions and "he shook his raiment, and said unto them, Your blood be upon your own heads; I am clean: from henceforth I will go unto the Gentiles" (Acts 18:6). His frustration led him to hold separate meetings from the local congregation of Jews, probably the first distinctly Christian meeting of members other than the small meetings held by the missionaries in the city. The result of this action, which had been inspired by Paul's frustration, was that "Crispus, the chief ruler of the synagogue" converted to the Lord, together "with all his house" (Acts 18:8). The chief ruler of a synagogue was equivalent to a bishop in Christian tradition, and many would interpret his conversion as showing that the missionaries taught the true gospel. The conversion of the local bishop led to the second major event Luke records.

The local Jews, sensing that the Christian missionaries were making inroads into their congregation, complained of Paul to the local governor Gallio. Hoping perhaps to have Paul banished from the city, they presented a trumped-up charge of treason, which Gallio saw through immediately. The accusation brought against Paul read, "This fellow persuadeth men to worship God contrary to the law" (Acts 18:13). Luke, whose loose wording could mean that they complained that Paul taught against Roman or Jewish law, portrays the charge as one that would be of interest to a Roman court. However, Gallio dismissed it as "a question of words and names, and of your law" (Acts 18:15). His statement that it is a matter of "your law" gives the impression that they had tried to convince him that it was really a matter of Roman law. The question "of words and names" is a clear reference to the argument being carried on between Christians who taught that Jesus Christ was the Messiah and Jews who believed in a Messiah but did not believe that Jesus fulfilled that prophecy. Part of the confusion lies in the fact that "Christ" is the linguistic equivalent of "Messiah," but whether he was *The Messiah* was an issue of intense debate.

Luke's account of the events that followed Gallio's decision to dismiss the charges raises questions about the branch of the church in Corinth. According to the report, "the Jews made insurrection with one accord against Paul," but when the decision went against them, "all the Greeks took Sosthenes, the [new] chief ruler of the synagogue, and beat him before the judgment seat" (Acts 18:12, 17). It is unclear if Luke's tidy division between Jews and Greeks is a division within the synagogue or whether it is somehow meant to indicate that "all the Greeks" of the city attacked the leader of the synagogue because he had instigated a petty charge against Paul, whom they had come to admire through his teachings. Whether those Greeks who had converted to the gospel were in any way involved in the beating of Sosthenes is unclear, although it is evident that public opinion of the synagogue and its leaders had turned surprisingly anti-Jewish. Not only did the public openly persecute the leader of the synagogue, but also Gallio, the governor, did nothing to stop them. In any case, Luke's details about Paul's ministry in Corinth point to the conclusions that the local

Jewish congregation lost many members due to the conversion of the synagogue leader and that public opinion of the Jews reached a low point as they tried to lash out at those responsible for converting their members.

For probably the first time during the second mission, Paul's missionary efforts in a particular city came to a natural rather than forced ending. Prior to Corinth, Paul had been run out of every city in which he preached, sometimes under threat of death, and other times under suspicion, intrigue, and following severe persecution. Both Paul and Luke agree that the work in Corinth came to a point where "Paul after this [the accusation before Gallio] tarried there yet a good while, and then took his leave of the brethren, and sailed thence into Syria, and with him Priscilla and Aquila" (Acts 18:18). Paul was satisfied with the progress of the branch in Corinth, and therefore he departed with his small band of missionary companions in the direction of Syria (Antioch).

PAUL'S VOW

Luke reports that Paul, prior to departing for Antioch (or perhaps his home in Tarsus), "having shorn his head in Cenchrea: for he had a vow" departed by sea to Ephesus (Acts 18:18). It is assumed generally that Paul's vow was a Jewish Nazarite vow taken earlier in his ministry and completed just prior to his departure for Ephesus. The Nazarite vow was a temporary covenant between the member and the Lord during which time certain foods and practices would be avoided so that the person could come closer to God. Fasting often accompanied the Nazarite vow, and the Old Testament uses the term "separation" when describing the duration of it. As part of the vow, the Old Testament directs that "all the days of the vow of his separation there shall no razor come upon his head: until the days be fulfilled, in the which he separateth himself unto the Lord, he shall be holy, and shall let the locks of the hair of his head grow" (Numbers 6:5). Josephus confirms that first-century practice was very similar: "Moreover, when any have made a sacred vow, I mean those that are called Nazarites, that suffer their hair to grow long, and use no wine, when they consecrate their hair, and offer it for a sacrifice, they are to allot that hair for the priests [to be thrown into the fire]" (*Antiquities*, 4.5.4).

When Paul entered into a Nazarite vow is unknown, but it probably came during his stay in Corinth. Luke, who did not draw attention to the distinct Jewish background of the vow, wanted his audience to be aware that Paul had undergone such a vow, although he was unaware why he did so. Given that Paul's stay in Corinth had been the most positive missionary experience in his life thus far, it is likely that Paul took the vow as a sign of thanks for the bounteous harvest there and for the homes that had been opened to him. The story also says something of the religion of Paul, who is shown here to be profoundly and personally religious. Another clue in Luke's narrative may indicate that Paul was deeply grateful for Priscilla and Aquila,

The opulence of Ephesus can be appreciated in this photograph of a pedestrian pathway that is made entirely from mosaic tiles. Paul would have traveled along this street to visit the local shops.

who now traveled with him to Ephesus. The couple apparently had some personal wealth, and although they worked and lived in Corinth, they were able to travel quite freely (Acts 18:3). They became close friends and associates with Paul, and may even have helped finance his missionary travels.

The logical place to conclude such a vow was in Jerusalem, where "he shall offer his offering unto the Lord, one he lamb of the first year without blemish for a burnt offering, and one ewe lamb of the first year without blemish for a sin offering, and one ram without blemish for peace offerings, and a basket of unleavened bread, cakes of fine flour mingled with oil, and wafers of unleavened bread anointed with oil, and their meat offering, and their drink offerings" (Numbers 6:14–15). These offerings were to be made in the temple, where the sacrifices signified the end of the vow and where the participant would "shave the head" (Numbers 6:18). Luke seems to understand that Paul's vow was closely associated with a trip to the temple, and therefore concludes immediately after reporting that Paul had taken a vow by him saying, "I must by all means keep this feast that cometh in Jerusalem" (Acts 18:21). The trip to Jerusalem would offer Paul the opportunity to end his vow and report on his mission.

When the practice of taking Nazarite vows began to wane is uncertain, but it probably coincides with the destruction of the Jerusalem temple. For the first few generations of those converts who had been practicing Jews prior to becoming Christian, the taking of a Nazarite vow was relatively common. The practice most likely fell victim to misunderstanding, as more and more gentile converts no longer understood its purpose and origin.

EPHESUS

Travel by sea was precarious in the first century, although sea traffic had increased considerably in the Mediterranean after Rome's effort to suppress piracy and with technological improvements of commercial sailing vessels. The fear of sea travel is captured in this early statement: "For instance as to myself, when I am on a voyage and look down on the deep sea, or look round on it and see no land, I am out of my mind and imagine that I must drink up all this water if I am wrecked, and it does not occur to me that three pints are enough [if I am forced to drink it all down]" (Epictetus, *Works*, 2.16). Many in the first century felt that there were certain health benefits to sea travel as expressed in one account: "There are besides many other uses, the chief however being a sea voyage for those attacked by consumption, as I have said, and for haemoptysis [a bronchial hemorrhage], such as quite recently within our memory was taken by Annaeus Gallio after his consulship. Egypt is not chosen for its own sake, but because of the length of the voyage" (Pliny, *Natural History*, 31.33). Paul could easily have taken the land route back to Antioch and Jerusalem, but chose rather to travel first to Jerusalem by sea. He may have chosen this route simply because it was the quickest way to be at Jerusalem by Passover, but it also may have offered some hope of relief for his physical suffering. At the beginning of his final mission, Paul began to speak of his physical malady with increasing frequency, suggesting that he was experiencing growing pain and discomfort from it.

His stop in Ephesus was merely a resting point for the crew of the ship and a chance to either unload or take in cargo. Luke's account opens the possibility that Paul was in the city for a few weeks, but not much longer. Expecting to return quickly to Ephesus, Paul left his traveling companions—Priscilla and Aquila—there while he traveled on to Jerusalem.

The ministry of the apostle John has historically been linked with Ephesus. Eusebius, writing in the fourth century, passes on the tradition that "the holy apostles and disciples of our Saviour were scattered over the whole world. Thomas, tradition tells us, was chosen for Parthia, Andrew for Scythia, John for Asia, where he remained till his death at Ephesus" (Eusebius, *Church History,* 3.1). If the tradition that John taught the gospel in Ephesus and later moved there permanently is correct, then it is likely that he was already there when Paul arrived in the city in the mid-50s. Luke confirms that Paul was well received there, unlike many of the cities he had previously visited, suggesting that John may have already made many converts. Paul made a favorable impression on the city's inhabitants, who asked him to remain with them.

THE REPORT FROM THESSALONICA ARRIVES

Sometime after Paul's arrival in Ephesus but before he began his third mission, Paul received news that the rigorists in Thessalonica were trying to lead the members there astray by teaching false doctrines. The situation at Thessalonica was urgent. Between his departure from Thessalonica and his arrival in Ephesus, a member of the branch had written letters claiming that the Second Coming was much nearer than any of them had anticipated. This other letter writer may even have forged his letters in the name of an apostle, possibly Paul, as Paul seems to imply when he says, "Be not soon shaken in mind, or be troubled, neither by spirit, nor by word, *nor by letter as from us*" (2 Thessalonians 2:2; emphasis added).

This other letter writer caused Paul serious concern, eliciting from him a serious rebuke. Of the other letter writer, Paul wrote, "And to you who are troubled rest with us, when the Lord Jesus shall be revealed from heaven with his mighty angels, in flaming fire taking vengeance on them that know not God, and that obey not the gospel of our Lord Jesus Christ: Who shall be punished" (2 Thessalonians 1:7–9). At the conclusion of the epistle, Paul writes that the members should not associate

Paul visited Ephesus at the end of his second missionary journey. John the apostle also visited the city, which may explain Paul's warm reception there. These homes were uncovered off the main thoroughfare—Curetes Street. These homes belonged to the wealthy and upper class in Ephesus. In the center of the photo is the inner courtyard, with facilities used for cooking. The rooms of the house surround this inner courtyard.

with the "disorderly" and that they should withdraw from their company (2 Thessalonians 3:6, 11). Whoever these disorderly members were, their relationship to the other letter writer remains unclear. Whether they had adopted his teachings as their own or he was one of them is not stated in Paul's epistles. Paul seems to link the two, which suggests that whoever reported to him about problems in Thessalonica believed that the two were the same.

The exact nature of their heresy was in interpreting the nearness of the Second Coming as an opportunity to act badly, quitting their jobs and relying on the diligence of others for their support. It may even have been that they had quit their jobs in some misguided attempt to build a society founded on the law of consecration, hoping that others within the branch would soon join them. Paul undermines any such thinking with his directive that "if any would not work, neither should he eat. For we hear that there are some which walk among you disorderly, working not at all, but are busybodies" (2 Thessalonians 3:10–11). Rather than outline all of their doctrinal misunderstandings, Paul cut to the heart of the matter by teaching that the Second Coming was still distant and would not happen until there was first a "falling away" or an "apostasy" as Paul would have referred to it in Greek (2 Thessalonians 2:3). Without the concept of an immediate apostasy, whatever the nature of their heresy, their beliefs and claims simply did not make sense.

Paul also associated their heresy with the opposition that would arise in the latter days. In the latter days the "Wicked [will] be revealed, whom the Lord shall consume with the spirit of his mouth, and shall destroy with the brightness of his coming. . . . And with all deceivableness of unrighteousness in them that perish; because they received not the love of the truth, that they might be saved. And for this cause God shall send them strong delusion, that they should believe a lie" (2 Thessalonians 2:8–11). If God would destroy those who will believe a lie in the future, then would he not destroy those who believe one and perpetuate it now? Paul makes it clear that associating with these "disorderly" brethren could lead to an uncomfortably warm, fiery end.

From 2 Thessalonians we also learn that Timothy and Silas were still with Paul, proving to be some of his most trusted associates. They had remained with him except for a brief few weeks when he sent them back to Thessalonica to report on matters there. Timothy likely remained behind in Ephesus so that he could return to his home in Lystra while Silas traveled with Paul to Jerusalem, where his home was. Silas, after his return to Judea, drops entirely from Luke's narrative, while Timothy joins with Paul again during Paul's final mission.

PAUL'S OUTLOOK

This mission, like the previous one, was a time of development for Paul. In it, we see our first glimpses into the spiritual transformation taking place within Paul. He began this mission with grave concerns over how the policy concerning Gentiles who converted to Christianity would affect the members in those areas where he had previously taught the gospel. He seems to have been excited about the prospects for explosive growth in the regions of the first mission, and he and Barnabas initially set out to cover all of the cities that they had previously visited. At the start of this mission, however, Paul experienced what he felt was a major setback in the proselytizing of Gentiles. Peter, along with Barnabas, had offended some gentile members of the church when they refused to eat with them. Paul felt that they had allowed themselves to be swayed by false brethren who claimed to represent James. Paul, it seems, felt that this event effectively closed the door to missionary work in the neighboring regions—the areas where he taught the gospel during his mission with Barnabas.

Hoping to swing back into those same regions from the north, Paul had a vision in which he was directed to go into Macedonia, where he would teach the gospel for the first time in Europe. His efforts in Macedonia produced enemies and converts, and even though Paul was forced to flee to Athens to protect himself, he also established strong branches of the church in Philippi and Thessalonica. Athens proved to be a difficult city in which to preach the gospel, so Paul traveled to Corinth to spread the gospel. He had greater success in Corinth than in any other city, causing him to stay there for a year and a half. At the end of his stay there, after having established a branch of the church and having trained leaders, Paul traveled back to Jerusalem hoping to fulfill a Nazarite vow he had taken earlier.

The duration of this mission was most likely two to three

years. Previous to Corinth, Paul stayed only a short while in each city. He may have stayed in some cities for as little as two to three weeks. Roughly twenty years had passed since his vision on the road to Damascus, and Paul had served as a missionary for nearly half that time. The other half of his time was spent in quiet service in the branches near his hometown, where the greatness of his character was quietly refined.

The few letters that survive from this mission (Galatians and 1–2 Thessalonians) reveal that Paul's spiritual identity was still undergoing transformation. In nearly all of his letters during his mission to Asia, Greece, and Macedonia, Paul seemed to focus on himself as an example worthy of emulation. Perhaps inspired or discouraged by Peter's example in Antioch, Paul, who had previously thought himself blameless, found no difficulty in recommending his own example. The difficulty with these statements is not whether Paul was truly exemplary, but that he was subtly shifting attention away from Christ and the proper channels of priesthood authority.

Another aspect of Paul's developing spiritual identity is a growing dislike for internal dissension in the branches of the church. The rigorists, who continually tried to impose a form of converted Judaism on gentile converts, became a thorn in Paul's side. He slowly began to develop a detailed response to these rigorists, which eventually included the details of his faith versus grace discourse to the Romans at the end of his final mission.

Paul also learned a valuable lesson as he experienced significant health concerns, teaching him the Lord's lesson that external or physical trials perfect while internal persecution corrupts. His health issues helped shape and refine his character, as did an unjust imprisonment in Philippi. The internal dissensions in Thessalonica, however, threatened to tear the branch apart and produce a deviant and misguided strand of

Christianity that could ultimately infect other branches of the church in the region. Paul was cautiously aware of how the example of the Thessalonian saints was seen by all of those in Macedonia. If that branch of the church began teaching and perpetuating heretical doctrines, then their example would immediately infect other smaller branches of the church.

While these internal dissensions in the branches of Galatia and Thessalonica blossomed, Paul suffered silently with his own health concerns. During his final mission he began to curb those feelings of self-advertisement, perhaps a result of becoming increasingly aware of his own mortality. Paul probably celebrated his fiftieth birthday sometime in the last part of this mission or during the early part of his final mission, and his personal hopes began to shift toward the glorious resurrection of his own weakened physical body.

Only once during this mission did Paul refer to himself as an apostle, and in that instance he was clear that he was not "an apostle . . . of men, neither by man, but by Jesus Christ, and God the Father" (Galatians 1:1). In both of the epistles to the saints in Thessalonica, Paul made no mention of his call to the apostleship. His only claim was that God had appeared to him, thereby making him a witness to the resurrection and by definition an apostle. At the beginning of his final mission Paul reports that he was "called to be an apostle of Jesus Christ through the will of God" (1 Corinthians 1:1). In this instance he refers for the first time to a "call" rather than an appearance as the event that made him an apostle.

The mission to Asia, Greece, and Macedonia taught Paul about himself, and while he would continue throughout his life to deal with the ramifications of his previous assumptions of blamelessness, a dramatic shift took place in his thinking during his final mission. He had always placed Christ at the center of his teachings, but at times he had placed his own example between the members and Christ, understanding that his own example and works, which had led him to Christ, would also lead others to Christ. During his final mission, Paul would come to understand that his own suffering in the cause of Christ could help to sanctify him, if he responded to those sufferings in holiness. His new challenge was to convince all members that receiving the benefit of Christ's sufferings—meaning partaking of the blessings of his atonement—put one on the pathway to eternal exaltation.

Chapter 7

PAUL'S FINAL MISSION

"Without regard for personal comfort or safety, he traveled over the known world of his time, declaring that 'neither death, nor life, nor angels, nor principalities, nor powers, nor things present, nor things to come, nor height, nor depth, nor any other creature, shall be able to separate us from the love of God, which is in Christ Jesus our Lord' (Romans 8:38–39)."
—Gordon B. Hinckley

In Luke's account of the missions of Paul there is hardly any pause between his first trip to Corinth and his return there during his final mission. For Luke the two missions appear to be a single extended mission with a trip to Jerusalem and a stay in Antioch squeezed in between them. In fact, Luke does not differentiate between the two missions in any way other than Paul revisiting the areas he had previously visited. In Luke's eyes, Paul's entire postconversion life was an extended mission to Asia, Macedonia, and Greece, from which he never really came home. Given that Luke was a traveling companion of Paul, it is likely that his viewpoint was similar to the way Paul told the story.

Between his trip to Jerusalem and traveling to the first

major stop of his final mission—Ephesus—Paul wrote a letter to the saints living in Corinth. That letter, which precedes the two existing letters to Corinth and is now lost, is summarized in a single verse, "I wrote unto you in an epistle not to company with fornicators" (1 Corinthians 5:9). The lost letter to the Corinthians, from Paul's description of it, appears to have been a circular type of letter announcing a churchwide policy on some matter. Paul's reference to its contents has some similarity to the wording of the decision made at the Jerusalem council, which decided to require all Gentiles to "abstain . . . from fornication" (Acts 15:20). The letter was certainly written after Paul's visit there, and hence several years after the decision of the Jerusalem council, but the exact reasons why he chose to remind them of the council's decision so late is unclear.

The circular letter was probably inspired by Paul's reports in Jerusalem of his missionary successes. The rigorists there again became concerned that he was perverting the law of Moses, so in order to calm their concerns, he wrote a short letter reminding the Gentiles (i.e., Corinthians) of what the council had previously decided. Those who were concerned about Paul's missionary activities in the gentile regions of the Mediterranean would later lay a plot at the end of his final missionary journey that would result in his arrest.

A CRISIS DEVELOPS IN EPHESUS

Before his arrival in Ephesus, Paul revisited the cities in Galatia and Phrygia where he had traveled with Barnabas. Luke makes no mention of any specific activity in those areas; he refers to them only in passing as he narrates Paul's travels toward the Aegean Sea. On his mission to Asia, Greece, and Macedonia, Paul became frustrated at the lack of interest demonstrated by the inhabitants of those cities, associating their indifference with the events that had transpired in Antioch. In passing through Antioch on his way to Ephesus, Paul strengthened the faithful in those cities, but again realizing he had few opportunities to teach the gospel there, he quickly headed west.

As Paul and others were teaching the gospel in the northern Mediterranean, an active mission was also developing in North Africa. That mission, particularly Alexandria in Egypt, has been associated, since at least the fourth century, with Mark the author of the second gospel. This same Mark is also linked with Peter in the same sources, indicating perhaps that Peter may have directly supervised the missionary work there. Whatever the case, as in other areas of the church, the Jews were the first to respond to the gospel message: "And a certain Jew named Apollos, born at Alexandria" heard the gospel and converted (Acts 18:24). The fifth-century manuscript (Bezae Catabrigiensis) relates that Apollos heard the gospel in "his native country." Whether the mission in North Africa was beset by factionalism or heresy is difficult to ascertain; however, Apollos, who was taught the gospel there, had only been taught "the baptism of John" (Acts 18:25). What type of missionary would teach him the gospel but not direct him to someone who could bestow the gift of the Holy Ghost is unclear, but not long after his conversion Apollos traveled to Corinth to continue preaching the gospel there.

Apollos likely traveled out of North Africa with other converts who made their way into Ephesus, where Paul encountered them. Paul seems to have been unconcerned about Apollos but greatly concerned over the handful of converts who, like Apollos, had only been baptized "unto John's baptism" (Acts 19:3). As his first surviving letter to the Corinthian saints attests, they had been visited by Peter during this time. Perhaps Paul's fears were allayed when he realized that Peter was there to confer the gift of the Holy Ghost on Apollos. The need to arrive in Ephesus quickly and stem any potential heresy or schism created by these new converts who had "not so much as heard whether there be any Holy Ghost" seems to explain why Paul moved hurriedly through the cities of Lystra, Derbe, Pisidian Antioch, and so on (Acts 19:2). The only city in the region where a visit can be confirmed is Lystra, where he picked up Timothy, who had gone back to his hometown at the end of the previous mission to visit his family. If Luke's chronology for this period is accurate, then the visit was short-lived.

The North African members, upon hearing the gospel taught in its fullness, "were baptized in the name of the Lord Jesus. And when Paul had laid his hands upon them, the Holy Ghost came on them. . . . And all the men were about twelve" (Acts 19:5–7). Luke's careful wording of their baptism may suggest that the North African mission was facing greater issues than simply not conferring the gift of the Holy Ghost upon all converts. Paul had to rebaptize those members "in the name of Lord Jesus," apparently, as Luke tells the story, because they had been baptized unto "John."

After rebaptizing these dozen or so members, Paul seems to have settled into tranquility in Ephesus, teaching the gospel at the school of Tyrannus (Acts 19:9). During his previous journey through Ephesus, Paul was openly welcomed by the disciples there. However, on his return trip to the city, his powerful teaching led to a decisive break with the local synagogue, and "he departed from them [the synagogue], and separated the disciples" (Acts 19:9). This is one of the few places that specifically mentions that Christians met alongside Jews for some time, prior to "separating" themselves from the synagogue. This rupture with the synagogue led to further difficulties for Paul and his companions, a result of the local leadership being offended at the departure of a portion of their membership.

LUKE'S PERSPECTIVE ON PAUL'S STAY IN EPHESUS

Luke provides more information about Paul's stay in Ephesus than about any other city he visited, although he spends more time on his arrest and imprisonment at Caesarea than on any other single period of the apostle's life. For some reason, Luke gave a more detailed report of Paul's work in Ephesus, even though he likely had great success in Philippi and Corinth. As Luke tells the story, Paul's ministry in Ephesus became less and less palatable to some of the local inhabitants, eventually leading both the local Jewish congregation and the gentile inhabitants of the city to oppose his work.

Additionally, Luke records that "vagabond Jews, exorcists" tried to use the power of the priesthood after having seen Paul rebuke spirits in the name of Jesus (Acts 19:13). Luke was not certain if these were local riffraff who opposed Paul or whether these were literally "vagabond" Jews traveling the countryside who had encountered Paul in this new setting. Luke was only aware that their misguided attempt to use the priesthood ultimately led to the conversion of many who witnessed it. The sons of Sceva attempted to cast an evil spirit out of a man possessed (Acts 19:14), but were not fully aware of what they were doing. This led to the possessed man turning on them and wounding them. The result of this priesthood experiment was that "this was known to all the Jews and Greeks also dwelling at Ephesus; and fear fell on them all, and the name of the Lord Jesus was magnified. And many that believed came, and confessed, and shewed their deeds" (Acts 19:17–18).

Unfortunately, Luke does not seem to be aware of another logical outcome of his account, because it could easily have been interpreted in the opposite way. By using the "name of the Lord Jesus," a certain group of miscreant Jews brought about either their own demonic possession or their being overpowered by evil spirits. An outsider's viewpoint might consider the event to be a result of using Jesus' name. Without understanding proper priesthood authority, the story could easily be interpreted either way. Implied in the story is the fact that Paul healed either the possessed man, or the sons of Sceva, and that a large gathering was present to hear the possessed man proclaim, "Jesus I know, and Paul I know; but who are ye?" (Acts 19:15). Luke tells the story as a positive missionary experience, one that led to the conversion of many in the city. The difficulty is that often such dramatic missionary experiences are accompanied by equally dramatic periods of persecution or opposition.

Toward the end of his stay in Ephesus, Paul sent Timothy and Erastus into Macedonia ahead of him, probably hoping to ascertain whether a trip to Thessalonica would be advisable. He had previously been forced out of the city, but then written two epistles to the saints there. Timothy, who had been welcome in the city even after Paul was forced out, traveled back to the area with Erastus from Corinth to see what effect Paul's letters had

This stone inscription is one of the few surviving artifacts that refers directly to one of Paul's traveling companions. The inscription, found near the theater in Corinth, reads, "Erastus, commissioner of public works (aedile), laid this pavement at his own expense." Paul mentioned Erastus from Corinth in his epistle to the Romans, although he called him the city "chamberlain" (Romans 16:23).

on the saints there. Paul records that Timothy's eventual destination was Corinth (1 Corinthians 4:17). It is in this context that Luke first records Paul's plans to visit Rome: "After these things were ended, Paul purposed in the spirit, when he had passed through Macedonia and Achaia, to go to Jerusalem, saying, After I have been there, I must also see Rome" (Acts 19:21).

Underlying the decision to preach the gospel in Rome was an inspired prompting, and Paul, perhaps realizing what lay ahead of him, determined to avoid any further persecution in the region so that he could safely fulfill the mission the Spirit had whispered to him. Unfortunately, his experiences in Ephesus would detain him for a season and lead to a dramatic change in his outlook.

PAUL WRITES TO CORINTH

While staying in Ephesus and teaching at the school of Tyrannus, Paul received both a letter and an oral report from Chloe, a member of the branch in Corinth, detailing problems that had developed after his departure. Paul had not been away from the city for very long, but some members of the branch had begun indulging in unholy practices and teaching false doctrines. Paul responded by writing 1 Corinthians, with chapters 1 through 6 answering the oral report Chloe had delivered and chapters 7 through 16 answering point by point the details of the written letter she had brought. In looking at the first epistle in this manner, it is apparent that the saints there had drafted a formal letter detailing their doctrinal and practical concerns, which was either transmitted under Chloe's name or written by her. Their other concerns, which were communicated by Chloe, detail some of the issues she felt had led to the schism in Corinth, as well as a few general issues facing the branch.

The saints in Corinth asked for Paul's opinions on the statement, "It is good for a man not to touch a woman," on whether the saints could eat meat that had been previously used in a sacrifice to a pagan deity, on whether Paul was an apostle, on the need for baptism, on local customs of hairstyles and grooming, on the sacrament, on the manifestation of spiritual gifts, on the resurrection of the dead, and on the collection for the poor saints in Jerusalem (1 Corinthians 7:1; 8:4; 9:1; 10:1–11:34; 12:1–14:40; 15:1–58; 16:1–2).

Chloe's oral report detailed an underlying tension in the branch concerning the superiority of whichever person had administered their saving ordinances. Some in the branch felt that they were better than others because they had been baptized by Peter, Apollos, or Paul. Chloe appears to have reported a private concern that the members were beginning to delve into mysteries or matters inappropriate for newly baptized members. Her final concern, the most scandalous, was that a young man had married his stepmother, probably after the death of his father. Given the ages at which couples were married in the first century, usually before they were twenty but at times as young as twelve and thirteen, it is not impossible that this young man was only a few years younger than his stepmother. Chloe was scandalized by the affair, and sought Paul's direction on how the branch should proceed in dealing with this situation.

Paul's response, now referred to as 1 Corinthians but actually the second letter written to the branch there, contains a careful response to both Chloe's written and oral reports. Paul was cautious not to undermine his work in the city; therefore he was careful in his epistle to instruct as well as correct, not wanting to become overbearing to the newly formed branch leadership.

THE DIVISION IN CORINTH

Below the surface of Paul's letter is an underlying tension with factionalism in the branch in Corinth. Having heard the report from Chloe, Paul seems to have been immediately prompted to visit the city and repair any damage resulting from divisions in the branch. The earliest complete codex (manuscript book) of Paul's letters contains the word "division" instead of "divisions" as in many modern bibles (1 Corinthians 1:10); the singular is historically more accurate. Paul's later statements in the epistle confirm either that someone had followed Paul to Corinth and begun teaching against Paul in order to undermine his achievements there or one of the local members had led away some members in a doctrinal revolt against the apostle's teachings.

Unlike the opposition he had experienced from Jewish rigorists in Judea, Antioch, and Galatia, the Corinthian disaffection came from a perversion of doctrine. Perhaps at the heart of the problem was the teaching, "Now if Christ be preached that he rose from the dead, how say some among you that there is no resurrection of the dead?" (1 Corinthians 15:12). Not only would such a teaching undermine the gospel of Christ, it would also undercut Paul's vision on the road to Damascus and his apostleship. If Christ had not resurrected, then Paul could not have seen him. This may be one of the reasons that Paul began this letter, unlike his previous letters, with a reminder that he had now been "called to be an apostle" (1 Corinthians 1:1). The challenge to Paul's apostleship is manifest indirectly in his rejoinder: "Am I not an apostle. . . . If I be not an apostle unto others, yet doubtless I am to you" (1 Corinthians 9:1–2).

For whatever reason, some of the saints in Corinth had begun to look at Paul's service among them with a more critical eye. They challenged his calling and his vision on the road to Damascus, some of them making comparisons to other known apostles. Some of the old Paul reemerges in his denunciation of those who had opposed him. A negative comparison between apostles who were financially supported by the church and Paul, who worked with his own hands, appears to have generated the discussion. These detractors claimed that because Paul worked among them he was not really an apostle of the Lord and that such lowly manual labor and artisan-class skills were evidence enough he was not equal in stature to the other apostles. His retort is that he had the ability to ask for assistance from the branches, but he chose to work among them to be an example. He taught, "Mine answer to them that do examine me is this, Have we not power to eat and to drink? Have we not power to lead about a sister, a wife, as well as other apostles, and as the brethren of the Lord [Jesus' earthly brothers], and Cephas? . . . If others be partakers of this power over you, are not we rather? Nevertheless we have not used this power; but suffer all things, lest we should hinder the gospel of Christ. . . . The Lord ordained that they which preach the gospel should live [financially] of the gospel" (1 Corinthians 9:3–14). The issue was not whether Paul could ask for financial support from the members, but whether he chose not to, and therefore he argued that others who did not have either the ability or time to earn their own living should not be used to disparage Paul's practice of working to provide for himself.

The other major source feeding the growing disaffection in Corinth is evident in one of the questions contained in Chloe's letter. In it, the saints had asked whether it was appropriate to eat meat that had been sacrificed to pagan deities. A simple straightforward response to such an apparently uncomplicated question would seem sufficient, but Paul saw something else in the question, and responded by saying: "We know that we all have knowledge. Knowledge puffeth up, but charity edifieth. And if any man think that he knoweth any thing, he knoweth nothing yet as he ought to know" (1 Corinthians 8:1–2). Paul's response implies that the issue of whether to eat meat that had been used in a sacrifice to a pagan deity was a result of a higher law–lower law mentality, which the apostle instantly recognized and rebuked. Instead of citing the precedent given at the Jerusalem council, which was that they should not eat "things strangled, and from blood," both of which were issues arising from meat used in sacrifices, Paul rebuked them for being puffed up because of their higher "knowledge" (Acts 15:20).

Unlike previous encounters with internal dissenters, Paul now faced a faction within the church that deprecated the resurrection, discounted his apostleship, and developed a higher-law mentality with which they sought to differentiate themselves from their fellow Christians who only lived the lower law.

Unfortunately the first letter to the Corinthian branch did little to settle the doctrinal disputes there, as the second letter attests. In the first epistle, Paul's focus was on settling misunderstandings that had arisen from the teaching of false doctrine. The first letter reveals that his intent was to teach them correct doctrine, which would in turn help bring the branch back into harmony with the church. However, as the second letter reveals, the disputes and misunderstandings continued to develop, and by the time that he wrote it, Paul recommended that the faithful saints in Corinth distance themselves from those who taught false doctrine and perpetuated false practice.

PAUL'S EPHESIAN IMPRISONMENT

Sometime during Paul's stay in Ephesus, probably towards the end, Paul faced terrible tribulation. Whatever the exact details of his trial there, it eventually led to a temporary imprisonment in the city. Luke records that Paul's missionary activities eventually led to a riot in the theater, where Demetrius the

This massive theater is located a short distance from the famous Temple of Diana (Artemis) at Ephesus and was also the site where Demetrius the silversmith led a riot against Christian missionaries who had converted some of the followers of Diana. Paul was able to escape harm, but his companions Aristarchus and Gaius were rushed into the theater and threatened by a mob.

silversmith led a group of rioters to protest Paul's attempt to convert the followers of the pagan deity Diana (Artemis) to Christianity. Some of the local members were successful in keeping Paul out of the fray, but the local artisans under Demetrius's spell arrested Gaius and Aristarchus, two of Paul's missionary companions (Acts 19:29). Luke did not record any subsequent threat to Paul's life as a result of this riot, but in Paul's later writings he referred to some terrible consequences of his ministry there.

In his letter to the saints in Corinth, Paul referred to an event he described thusly: "If after the manner of men I have fought with beasts at Ephesus, what advantageth it me, if the dead rise not? let us eat and drink; for to morrow we die" (1 Corinthians 15:32). Somewhat tongue in cheek, Paul explained that his true devotion to the gospel was manifest in the events that transpired in Ephesus, where he defended his life against "beasts." Were there no resurrection, what value would there have been in risking his life for the gospel's sake?

In a later letter—Philippians—Paul refers to an imprisonment in the "palace" and that his "bonds in Christ are manifest" (Philippians 1:13). The reference to the "palace" and the "praetorian guard" has led to the conjecture that this letter must have been written from a later Roman imprisonment, but the city of Ephesus was a haven for worship of the deified Roman emperor, with several temples surviving from the first and second centuries A.D. These references to the emperor's guard could equally refer to the authorities of the emperor's temple in the city, and therefore Paul's reference to an imprisonment may also refer to his incarceration in Ephesus.

It is also in this epistle that Paul begins to see his own death as a distinct, perhaps imminent, possibility: "Him therefore I hope to send presently, so soon as I shall see how it will go with me" (Philippians 2:23). Paul ponders his own demise, saying, "For to me to live is Christ, and to die is gain" (Philippians 1:21). Something in his recent experiences had led him to ask whether death would offer welcome relief.

The most powerful piece of evidence for an Ephesian imprisonment comes from 2 Corinthians where Paul makes explicit reference to a terrible ordeal that took place in Asia. Although he does not explicitly mention imprisonment as part of his suffering, he does say, "For we would not, brethren, have you ignorant of our trouble which came to us in Asia, that we were pressed out of measure, above strength, insomuch that we despaired even of life" (2 Corinthians 1:8). The phrase "pressed out of measure, above strength" could more literally be rendered "we were overcome, beyond our power to endure" to the point that they thought they would die from it.

Paul may have made a passing reference to the same event when he said, "For I think that God hath set forth us the apostles last, as it were appointed to death: for we are made a spectacle unto the world, and to angels, and to men" (1 Corinthians 4:9). The sense of Paul's statement is that God has tried and tested the apostles by appointing them to die for the word's sake; therefore, their lives and trials are literally presented to mankind on the stage of life, in a theater, as it were, so that all could witness their sufferings. If this reference is an allusion to the events that transpired in Ephesus, then the event must have had some broad public component or at least have been well publicized.

First-century descriptions of prison reveal that it was comparable in many ways to modern concepts of torture and abuse. Cicero relates that in a typical political imprisonment "no degree of the most terrible torture is omitted" (Cicero, *Orations,* 5.90).

In Roman times, prisoners were treated differently depending on social status and citizenship. According to Cicero, the initial treatment of prisoners was determined by whether they were Roman citizens or not (*Against Verres,* 2.5.61). The practice, which may have changed slightly in the centuries following Paul, was to send non-Romans into the arena to be eaten by wild animals, while Roman citizens were beheaded (Eusebius, *Church History,* 5.1.47). One particularly gruesome account demonstrates that those who were condemned to death were sometimes used in experiments (vivisection) so that physicians could understand more fully the human body (Celsus, *Prooemium,* 23–26).

The harrowing experience of being imprisoned was intended as a detriment to any future criminal activity for the accused or for any onlookers. Prisons were disease-infested torture chambers where the dregs of society were physically separated from the general populace and used as examples of the cause and effect relationship between criminal activity and death.

For Paul, his suffering in Ephesus became a Liberty Jail experience. Just as the Prophet Joseph Smith suffered tremendously in a Missouri jail, Paul suffered beyond measure in an Ephesian jail. At one point, the Prophet cried out, "O God, where art thou? And where is the pavilion that covereth thy hiding place? How long shall thy hand be stayed, and thine eye, yea thy pure eye, behold from the eternal heavens the wrongs of thy people and of thy servants, and thine ear be penetrated with their cries? Yea, O Lord, how long shall they suffer these wrongs and unlawful oppressions, before thine heart shall be softened toward them, and thy bowels be moved with compassion toward them?" (D&C 121:1–3). In those miserable conditions the Prophet Joseph Smith came to know God in a way that only his sufferings could teach him. He entered that jail a remarkable man, but he left that jail profoundly changed and more aware of the ramifications of his calling as the Prophet of the Restoration.

Orson F. Whitney described many of the similarities between Joseph Smith and Paul when he said: "I perused, not for the first time, the life of the Apostle Paul, reading along with it the epistles of St. Paul and the Acts of the Apostles. I was struck more forcefully than ever with the general similarity between the experiences of that great man, that mighty apostle of Jesus Christ, and the experiences of another great man, another mighty apostle of our Lord, namely, the Prophet Joseph Smith. I could almost imagine myself reading the history of the modern prophet while poring over the biography of the ancient apostle" (in Conference Report, October 1912, 68).

Paul had a similar experience in an Ephesian prison in the late 50s, and although his "Liberty Jail" epistle has not survived, his changed outlook can be easily documented. The change in thought from believing that he would be alive at the second coming to expecting his own death can be traced chronologically through his letters. In one of his first epistles Paul taught, "But I would not have you to be ignorant, brethren, concerning them which are asleep [dead], that ye sorrow not, even as others which have no hope. . . . For this we say unto you by the word of the Lord, that *we which are alive and remain unto the coming of the Lord* shall not prevent [precede] them which are asleep. . . . Then *we which are alive and remain* shall be caught up together with them in the clouds" (1 Thessalonians 4:13–17; emphasis added). Here Paul implies that some, including himself, would be alive at the second coming of Christ.

In his first epistle to the Corinthians he states, "Behold, I shew you a mystery; *We shall not all sleep* [die], but we shall all be changed" (1 Corinthians 15:51; emphasis added). This epistle was written around the time that he was imprisoned in Ephesus, and given his perspective in it, he likely wrote it before his terrible ordeal there. Not much later, after having experienced awful events in Ephesus, Paul wrote to the Philippian saints: "For to me to live is Christ, and to die is gain. But if I live in the flesh, this is the fruit of my labour: *yet what I shall choose I wot not.* For I am in a strait betwixt two, having a desire to depart [die], and to be with Christ; which is far better: Nevertheless to abide in the flesh is more needful for you" (Philippians 1:21–24; emphasis added). Between the two epistles Paul's outlook on his own demise had changed drastically. Prior to writing Philippians, he had always used "we" when referring to those who would be alive at Christ's second coming. However, in the letter to the saints in Philippi, he expressed for the first time the great advantage it would be to die and be with Christ.

Not long after writing to Philippi, and perhaps having experienced renewed symptoms from his thorn in the flesh, Paul wrote again to the saints in Corinth, stating, "For we know that if our earthly house of this tabernacle were dissolved, we have a building of God, an house not made with hands, eternal in the heavens. *For in this we groan, earnestly desiring to be clothed upon with our house which is from heaven. . . .* For we that are in this tabernacle do groan, being burdened: not for that we would be unclothed, but clothed upon, that mortality might be swallowed up of life" (2 Corinthians 5:1–4; emphasis added). This statement is very similar but more complete than an earlier one that he made to the Philippians where he said, "The Lord Jesus Christ: Who shall change our vile body, that it may be fashioned like unto his glorious body" (Philippians 3:20–21).

The event that appears to have most influenced his changing attitude towards his own death was the trial that he experienced in Ephesus. None of Paul's later letters contain any reference to "we" when referring to the Second Coming. Somewhere along the way he learned that he would no longer be alive when the Savior returned, but he would instead return in a glorious resurrected body, whose glory would surpass any earthly glory. He also seemed to anticipate some improvement in his physical body through the effects of the resurrection. His thorn in the flesh would be removed and he would enter the eternities unhindered.

Implied, although not expressed in these statements, is a comfort with his eternal standing. Many have feared death and resurrection, worrying that their eternal station might be less than they had hoped for. Such hesitancy is absent from Paul's statements. In his earlier statements he expected the Lord to greet him warmly at His coming, whereas his later references reveal a clear yearning to be with God and Christ, fully expecting that he will be welcomed in their embrace. Paul does not speak of his own salvation as the result of it having been promised to him, but rather that his faith and good works have generated an undying hope that God loves him. Such firm hope of salvation became his apostolic example to the branches of the church during his final missionary journey.

THE IMPRISONMENT EPISTLES

Sometime during his imprisonment in Ephesus, Paul wrote several letters to branches of the church detailing his concerns for their welfare and expressing a hope that he would not be detained long. These letters, therefore, may originate from the first part of Paul's imprisonment, when he still felt secure about his release.

The epistle to the Philippians reveals the inner torment of the apostle, who felt that rigorist tendencies within the branches were corrupting the gospel of Jesus Christ. Earlier Paul had been vociferous in denouncing the enemies of the church, but in this epistle he approached the problem by undermining both their doctrinal positions and carnal credentials.

To call attention to the fallacy of preaching by virtue of human credentials, Paul taught that his credentials were superior: "If any other man thinketh that he hath whereof he might trust in the flesh, I more: Circumcised the eighth day, of the stock of Israel, of the tribe of Benjamin, an Hebrew of the Hebrews; as touching the law, a Pharisee; concerning zeal, persecuting the church; touching the righteousness which is in the law, blameless" (Philippians 3:4–6). The phrase "Hebrew of the Hebrews" can mean simply a Jew born of Jewish progenitors, but it also reveals a superlative concept of lineage or, when taken in context, Paul boasts that he is the most qualified Hebrew among them, yet, "But what things were gain to me, those I counted loss for Christ" (Philippians 3:7). Lineage and credentials, or the claims of his opponents, were nothing when considered in the context of the eternities.

An inner turmoil also surfaces in the letter when Paul teaches, "not having mine own righteousness, which is of the law, but that which is through the faith of Christ, the righteousness which is of God by faith: That *I may know him, and the power of his resurrection,* and the fellowship of his sufferings, being made conformable unto his death; If by any means I might attain unto the resurrection of the dead. *Not as though I had already attained,* either were already perfect" (Philippians 3:9–12; emphasis added). Publicly, Paul acknowledged his imperfection in the context of opposition to his teachings. Earlier, Paul would have suppressed the opposition against his teachings with the hope that he could overwhelm his opponents; however, in this instance he refers to some of his own shortcomings and thus reveals a more humble side. He also reveals that he had received no promise of salvation, hoping that he would "attain unto the resurrection" or, in restoration terminology, attain to the first resurrection with Jesus Christ.

Part of his correspondence to the Philippians was to thank them for their voluntary financial support to him during his travels in Macedonia on his first visit there. It is likely that the funds they sent permitted him to travel to Athens ahead of the other missionaries, who had to work to earn enough money to travel there (Philippians 4:14–18). For their generosity, Paul warmly thanked the saints and invoked his blessing upon them.

During the same time period, Paul wrote a personal letter to Philemon concerning a runaway slave whom he had met in prison. Paul had the privilege of getting to know not only the runaway slave—Onesimus or "useful"—but also his master, Philemon. The letter shows a playful side of the apostle, who jokingly writes to Philemon, "I entreat you for Useful, my son, whom I have begotten during my imprisonment, who in times past was un-useful to you, but is now useful to you and I" (Philemon 1:10–11; author's translation). Moreover, Paul implores Onesimus's owner to be lenient on him when he returns, assuring Philemon that "if he hath wronged thee, or oweth thee ought, put that on mine account; I Paul have written it with mine own hand, I will repay it" (Philemon 1:18–19). This personal side of the apostle shows a good-spirited personality who can tease even though he faces the most awful consequences. Thus, the powerful personality of the 30s and 40s gives way to a gentler father figure who shows increasing love for those with whom he comes into contact.

PAUL'S RETURN TO GREECE

Luke collapses nearly the entire second half of the final mission into a few short verses, detailing Paul's return to Greece by saying, "And when he had gone over those parts, and had given them much exhortation, he came into Greece, and there abode three months" (Acts 20:2–3). Likely, Paul's concerns for the branch there inspired his trip into Greece. There was no way to tell whether his letter in response to the reports from Chloe had settled the division or whether it required a personal visit. The brevity of his trip through Macedonia (Philippi and Thessalonica) suggests either that Paul was still unwelcome there or that he found the branches there thriving. The latter possibility seems unlikely given the tenor of his letters to Philippi and Thessalonica.

As Paul returned from visiting Corinth, for which no report is given, he sent several of his missionary companions ahead of him to meet him when he arrived in Troas. He apparently chose a neutral city, having been driven out of and persecuted in the majority of cities he had visited thus far. Among those whom he sent ahead were Timothy and Trophimus, who would eventually travel with him to Jerusalem (Acts 20:4). At this point in the story, Luke reintroduces himself into the narrative, indicating that he sailed with Paul from Philippi to Troas to meet his brethren there (Acts 20:6). This is the same journey that Luke had taken previously and may indicate that he had remained in

Located south of the ancient city of Troy along the Mediterranean coastline, Alexander Troas was the place where Paul met with a small group of trusted friends and missionary companions prior to traveling to Jerusalem.

these parts for the duration of Paul's missions. Luke was likely from the area and served as a local missionary, never traveling with Paul further east into Greece.

A few weeks after Paul had sent his brethren ahead to meet him, Paul sailed with Luke to meet them in Troas. This preplanned rendezvous included some of his closest associates, men whom he planned to send back into the regions he had just visited. While the others set sail from Troas around the peninsula, Paul set out on foot, hoping to meet his dear friend Titus, whom he had asked to join him, between there and Assos. While journeying, Paul did meet with Titus, who had apparently been detained for only a short while. When the group traveling by sea met up with Paul in Assos, he boarded the ship with them and sailed toward Ephesus.

The apostle's great love for Titus is revealed in a touching remark he made to the branch at Corinth: "I had no rest in my spirit, because I found not Titus my brother" (2 Corinthians 2:13). He reflected later on the situation, saying, "For, when we were come into Macedonia, our flesh had no rest, but we were troubled on every side; without were fightings, within were fears. Nevertheless God, that comforteth those that are cast down, comforted us by the coming of Titus" (2 Corinthians 7:5–6). Paul immediately sent Titus back to Corinth to see how matters were developing there (2 Corinthians 8:6). Titus may have carried with him a portion of the letter that is now known as 2 Corinthians.

Why Paul was so worried about Titus's safety is unclear, but his account of the period reveals a deep concern that none of the missionaries was safe in those regions and that their only hope was to travel back to Jerusalem and from there depart for Rome. The sending of Titus to Corinth and Timothy and others ahead of him also demonstrates a deep concern for those branches of the church that he had helped establish, but sending the missionaries alone also shows that Paul himself would not travel there. Luke records that during this time period, Paul had become increasingly determined to travel to Jerusalem, leaving behind the cities of the Mediterranean seacoast. Luke, who probably reveals Paul's own publicly expressed opinions during the period in question, says that Paul was determined to be at Jerusalem by the time of the feast of Pentecost (near the beginning of May, literally fifty days after Passover). Even when members of the branch of Ephesus entreated him to stay and not go to Jerusalem he said, "But none of these things [threats on my life] move me, neither count I my life dear unto myself, so that I might finish my course with joy, and the ministry, which I have received of the Lord Jesus, to testify the gospel of the grace of God" (Acts 20:24).

PAUL WRITES TO CORINTH AGAIN

The history of Paul's Corinthian correspondence is complex. In all probability, the two letters that now survive contain fragments of the numerous letters that Paul wrote during his third missionary journey.

The letter now known as 2 Corinthians is likely a collection of several shorter letters written over a period of a year or more, after the major epistle (1 Corinthians) written in response to the reports delivered by Chloe. A quick glance at the epistle reveals that chapters eight and nine are nearly duplicate reports on the collection for the poor saints in Jerusalem. They may have originally been intended for two different congregations, possibly Corinth and Cenchrea, but could have been copied into a single document with other fragments of letters from Paul. In the letter itself Paul mentions several previous letters, which could either be references to portions of the first letter to Corinth or the second letter to Corinth. For example, he refers to a sorrowful letter: "For if I make you sorry, who is he then that maketh me glad, but the same which is made sorry by me? And *I wrote this same unto you*" (2 Corinthians 2:2–3; emphasis added) and "For though I made you sorry with a letter" (2 Corinthians 7:8). At some point, Paul's antagonists derided him, saying that his physical presence was weak, but his letters, of which we have only one previous surviving letter, are powerful, "For his *letters*, say they, are weighty and powerful" (2 Corinthians 10:10; emphasis added).

The reason that Paul stopped writing to the saints in Corinth is, however, more important than the details of which portion of which letter was written when. It appears that while Paul lived in Corinth, the missionary work flourished and the saints were well disposed toward him. However, not long after his departure, a small faction of members revolted against Paul's influence, disparaging him in light of the supposedly greater authority of Peter or the more persuasive speech of Apollos (1 Corinthians 1:11–13). The first letter to the saints there did not settle the dispute, and by the time Paul wrote the letters that would eventually be compiled into 2 Corinthians, it appears that the cancer of apostasy had spread.

Without doubt, the corruption worked its way from inside out, beginning with a small faction in the branch and spreading to other members. The first hint of doctrinal heresy in the branch can be seen in Paul's statement, "For *we are not as many,* which corrupt the word of God" (2 Corinthians 2:17; emphasis added). Who these "many" were is not yet clear, but they taught God in a corrupted fashion. The issue is brought to the surface later in the epistle when Paul says, "For if he that cometh preacheth *another Jesus,* whom we have not preached, or if ye receive *another spirit,* which ye have not received, or *another gospel,* which ye have not accepted, ye might well bear with him" (2 Corinthians 11:4; emphasis added). Someone was teaching "another Jesus" and "another gospel" by "another spirit." Paul's restraint in denouncing the offenders reveals his concern that the heresy might extend beyond the small group who had initially presented this new concept of Jesus.

These opponents came with letters of recommendation, which follow the standard practice of the day in proving important matters through the presentation of official documents that have been sealed and confirmed by witnesses. Such "letters," or more literally documents, were used to prove citizenship and to pass on important judicial decisions. Sarcastically, Paul denounces the practice of carrying letters of recommendation, which could easily be forged, saying, "Do we begin again to commend ourselves? or need we, as some others, epistles of commendation to you, or letters of commendation from you?" (2 Corinthians 3:1).

Paul's second question makes it apparent that he was not fully aware of the origin of these letters of recommendation; perhaps they were letters from a specific community commending the work of a particular missionary. Rather than being forged documents granting the bearer churchwide authority, the documents may have been letters of endorsement, recommending certain missionaries to neighboring branches. In this way the schism or doctrinal heresies of one community could be passed on without any overt intention at deception. One community could easily perpetuate a problem by endorsing a missionary who in turn passed on peculiar doctrinal teachings. Paul's later statement, that these teachers taught "another Jesus," would make more sense if this was the case in Corinth.

The nature of what they taught had a direct origin in Judaism and the law of Moses. In 2 Corinthians 3 and 4, Paul makes clear references to their beliefs, all of which betray a Jewish origin for the schism. For example, "Ye are manifestly declared to be the epistle of Christ . . . written . . . not in tables of stone," or more directly, "Who also hath made us able ministers of the new testament; not of the letter, but of the spirit: for the letter killeth, but the spirit giveth life. But if the ministration of death, written and engraven in stones, was glorious . . . How shall not the ministration of the spirit be rather glorious? For if the ministration of condemnation be glory, much more doth the ministration of righteousness exceed in glory" (2 Corinthians 3:3, 6–9).

The law of Moses is the background of their teachings, which Paul compares to beholding the fulness while wearing a veil (2 Corinthians 3:15). Paul is not disparaging the law of Moses itself, but the idea that the law of Christ should be made subservient to the law of the Old Testament. If one law should serve the other, then the law of Moses should become the servant of Jesus Christ, in whom exists the fulness. The consistent problem in the branches of the church in the 40s and 50s was that they faced an emotional struggle with not living both laws; their consciences, conditioned to the old law, would not permit them to move quickly.

Perhaps the most disconcerting issue in Paul's denunciation is his reference to these teachers as "false apostles" (2 Corinthians 11:13). Those in Corinth who claimed apostleship were certainly not claiming it as a calling, but rather by definition, for they like Paul had seen the resurrected Savior (1 Corinthians 15:6–7). Paul knew of more than five hundred individuals who became witnesses of the resurrection, thereby gaining instant recognition as authorities in the church. All of them, as Paul tells the story, were from Judea and Galilee and therefore rooted in the traditions of the law of Moses. There was probably not a single Gentile among them.

These authorities were a great asset in the missionary work of the church, but in some locales, they also became a hindrance as new members (Gentiles) continued to feel subservient to the more experienced members (Jews). In perhaps his most controversial epistle, Paul denounced some of these brethren, or those who claimed to represent them, as false brethren. Paul recognized that his approach was rude when he said, "But though I be rude in speech" (2 Corinthians 11:6). The greater good overcame his need to be polite, and answering the problems caused by these "chiefest apostles" was necessary if the branch was to be saved (2 Corinthians 11:5).

Some members of the Corinthian branch had already condemned Paul in their hearts. His response, in part, was to compare his own ministry to these false brethren and show that his was also legitimate, made more so through the sufferings that he had experienced. Calling them superlative apostles, Paul asked, "Are they Hebrews? so am I. Are they Israelites? so am I. Are they the seed of Abraham? so am I. Are they ministers of Christ? (I speak as a fool) I am more" (2 Corinthians 11:22–23).

For these brethren, for whom lineage was apparently more important than belief, Paul had very little patience. His patience wore particularly thin as a result of their repeated attacks on his apostleship after his departure. In each instance where Paul learned of the problems in Corinth, he had only recently departed from the city.

In this context Paul recounted the numerous trials and afflictions he had experienced as a missionary of Jesus Christ. To some this list may appear out of context, while to some it may appear that he may be legitimizing his apostleship by saying that he had suffered more than they (the false brethren) and therefore was more sincere in his ministry.

Something more profound is revealed in his list of afflictions and tribulations. He begins the list by saying, "in labours more abundant, in stripes above measure, in prisons more frequent, in deaths oft. Of the Jews five times received I forty stripes save one" (2 Corinthians 11:23–24). This list may appear to contain random acts of brutality that Paul suffered throughout his ministry, but as a Roman citizen Paul could not simply be beaten without trial. And in cases where he was injured by a mob, there would have certainly been consequences for those responsible.

Luke recorded differences in Paul's treatment by various mobs. When unjustly imprisoned and harshly treated in Philippi, Paul would not simply leave the city after his release. He wanted to make sure that the local officials understood that they had illegally mistreated him: "They have beaten us openly uncondemned, being Romans, and have cast us into prison; and now do they thrust us out privily? nay verily; but let them come themselves and fetch us out" (Acts 16:37). Later in Corinth, when Paul was unjustly accused before Gallio, the governor permitted the locals to abuse the person who had brought the unjust charges against Paul, showing a clear preference for Paul's rights over Sosthenes's (Acts 18:12–17). Up to this point, the only unjust imprisonment referenced in any of the histories is Paul's imprisonment in Philippi, yet in his second letter to the

Corinthians, Paul speaks of numerous trials, beatings, imprisonments, and so on.

The most intriguing reference in the list is, "Of the Jews five times received I forty stripes save one," which is a punishment Paul would have had to *willingly* accept from a local synagogue rather than it being a random act of persecution. Any punishment from Jews would have had to be coordinated with Roman authorities, a very unlikely historical scenario. When it is remembered that Paul recounted his list of trials in the context of Jewish opposition to his mission, it becomes apparent he was detailing not only his obedience to Christ but also his willing recognition of the authority of the local Jewish synagogues. His opponents had disparaged his ministry by saying that he was anti-Jewish, but Paul undermined those misguided accusations by testifying he had willingly accepted their punishments.

In the list, Paul also details other trials he faced: "In journeyings often, in perils of waters, in perils of robbers, in perils by mine own countrymen, in perils by the heathen, in perils in the city, in perils in the wilderness, in perils in the sea, in perils among false brethren; in weariness and painfulness, in watchings often, in hunger and thirst, in fastings often, in cold and nakedness" (2 Corinthians 11:26–27).

Unfortunately, no historical report is made of these trials and tribulations either by Paul or Luke; they are mentioned only as a counterattack to the claims of the false brethren in Corinth. The fact that Luke does not report the majority of these trials suggests that Paul did not speak of them or report them, making Paul's statement "I speak as a fool" stand out as sincere admission of embarrassment for ever having mentioned them.

Paul moves from his list of trials to speak of his vision of the third heaven, which given its current context would imply he included the report as an answer to the claims of heavenly visions by the false brethren at Corinth. His humility prohibited him from openly reporting that it was he who had seen the vision, in stark contrast to his willingness to recount his trials. He did not want to risk offending the Spirit of the Lord by revealing a sacred trust and thereby effectively close the heavens to himself in the future.

His report begins by providing the date of the vision, "fourteen years ago," which would place the vision during the time shortly prior to his first mission with Barnabas (2 Corinthians 12:2). Although Paul never reported the connection, it is possible that this vision signaled a transition in the apostle's life between the newly converted member serving as a missionary in his hometown and the great missionary to the Gentiles.

Paul was careful to not reveal anything of substance in his vision, indicating that he was making reference to it for reasons other than its contents alone. What he does report is that he was "caught up to the third heaven, . . . caught up into paradise, and heard unspeakable words, which it is not lawful for a man to utter" (2 Corinthians 12:2–4). The vision generated a feeling of pride in Paul, and to circumvent that, the Lord gave him a "thorn in the flesh, the messenger of Satan to buffet me, lest I should be exalted above measure. For this thing I besought the Lord thrice, that it might depart from me" (2 Corinthians 12:7–8). Earlier in his ministry, when he wrote to the Galatians, there was evidence that Paul's pride was placing roadblocks in the way of the ministry. It was also at that time that Paul began to speak of "a thorn in the flesh," and in this instance Paul provides a similar insight into why the Lord gave him such a trial: Paul's pride needed a counterbalance, a physical reminder of the power of the Lord.

The major difference between the writing of Galatians and 2 Corinthians is the change in Paul's personality. Second Corinthians shows a great degree of restraint on the part of

Paul, who could easily have lashed out at the false brethren, naming names, and denouncing those who associated with them as he had done following the event that transpired between Peter and Paul in Antioch (see Galatians 2). The report of the vision to the third heaven, which can be explained in part as a counter to the false brethren who claimed visions, may also have been part of a larger rebuttal of their claim that "his letters, say they [the false brethren], are weighty and powerful; but his bodily presence is weak" (2 Corinthians 10:10). Paul's bodily presence, deformed through "a thorn in the flesh," was God-given, a point that the apostle made to effectively end any further discussion of the matter. Some had made fun of his physical appearance, but after he had given the reason why he was now deformed, only the most hardened opponents would dare use it against him.

Paul had hoped to visit Corinth again, no doubt to ascertain whether his second epistle would have its desired effect. As a caring priesthood leader, he longed to see the dissensions there settled, the doctrinal disputes minimized, and the members returned to the true gospel of Jesus Christ. He told them that this is "the third time I am ready to come to you" (2 Corinthians 12:14). When he wrote the epistle he had visited Corinth on two occasions, but now he intended to travel to Jerusalem and then on to Rome. His proposed third visit was likely intended to be part of his journey to Rome, when he would have at least a brief opportunity to stop in the city to obtain a report on their well-being. This plan shows he thought he would go to Rome as a free man. When the time came, unbeknownst to him, he would go to Rome as a prisoner.

LUKE BEGINS HIS REPORT

"And when he met with us at Assos, we took him in, and came to Mitylene. And we sailed thence, and came the next day over against Chios; and the next day we arrived at Samos, and tarried at Trogyllium; and the next day we came to Miletus. For Paul had determined to sail by Ephesus, because he would not spend the time in Asia: for he hasted, if it were possible for him, to be at Jerusalem the day of Pentecost" (Acts 20:14–16). According to Luke, Paul was anxious to arrive in Jerusalem shortly after the Passover, but at the same time Luke did not report any apprehension on Paul's part concerning the opposition he would face there. As far as Luke was aware, Paul did not begin expressing doubts about his reception in Jerusalem until he met with the elders of Ephesus in Miletus.

Prior to his arrival in Miletus, Paul's outlook on his trip was apparently positive. But because of something he heard or of a prompting of the Spirit, he began to express worry that Jerusalem would become a negative experience. If his outlook was positive prior to Miletus and strained afterwards, then it is likely that he wrote both 2 Corinthians and Romans prior to his arrival there, for in both epistles he expresses a sincere optimism that he will leave Jerusalem a free man and be able to carry on his missionary travels. He had hoped to arrive in Rome and then eventually travel to Spain. Hebrews, on the other hand, was likely written after Miletus, when his outlook had changed and he began to have concerns about his well-being.

ROMANS

Unlike any of the previous letters that Paul had written, Romans was written to a community he had not visited or founded. He had heard of their faith—"your faith is spoken of throughout the whole world"—but he had never personally been in Rome (Romans 1:8). The community there was almost certainly founded by Peter, a tradition that dates back to the earliest accounts of Christianity after the apostolic era. Eusebius records, "The all-gracious and kindly providence of the universe brought to Rome to deal with this terrible threat to the world, the strong and great apostle, chosen for his merits to be spokesman for all the others, Peter himself" (*Church History*, 2.14). Paul did not intend to stay in Rome, but hoped to "take my journey into Spain . . . and to be brought on my way thitherward by you" (Romans 15:24). Rome was only a stopping place for Paul on his proposed mission to Spain, where the inhabitants spoke primarily Latin, thus offering a new challenge for preaching the gospel.

The city of Rome was a thriving metropolis in Paul's day, a city with a glorious veneer and rumors of vile corruption lying underneath. In one of Augustus's most famous self-aggrandizing moments he is reported to have said, "he so beautified it that he could justly boast that he had found it built of brick and left it in marble" (Suetonius, *The Lives of the Caesars*, 2.28). Such overstatements are contradicted by more cynical reports: "We inhabit a Rome for the most part supported by thin props. After all, that's how the agent blocks the buildings from falling down. Once he's covered a gaping ancient crack, he tells us not to worry, as we sleep in a building on the point of collapse" (Juvenal, *Satire*, 3).

Rome offered enticements of all kinds: "But the national morality, which had gradually fallen into oblivion, was being overthrown from the foundations by this imported licentiousness . . . and this at the instigation of the emperor and senate, who, not content with conferring immunity upon vice, were applying compulsion, in order that Roman nobles should pollute themselves on the stage under pretext of delivering an oration or a poem" (Tacitus, *Annals*, 14.20). Not unlike modern societies, the theater presented the extremes of public indecency.

Paul's purpose in going there may have been influenced by his concerns for the futurity of the missionary work in such a corrupt city. Certainly the branch there was strong, and Paul had probably heard of their faith. But the city was also a leader in vice, which made it problematic for the work of God to proceed. Paul had anticipated that the saints there would assist him financially in his missionary pursuits and therefore they were almost certainly well disposed toward the apostle when other cities had rejected him. The new frontier for Paul was in the west; he sensed that the opposition in the east had effectively ended his chances there.

Considering the difficulties that Paul faced during the latter half of his final mission, it is not surprising that he wrote a letter in his own defense. Previous letters had been written with the intent of settling doctrinal disputes, but Romans was written in order to alleviate any concerns that the saints might have about the content of Paul's teachings. Paul was concerned that teaching the gospel in areas where missionaries had already spread the gospel would engender strife: "I strived to preach the gospel, not where Christ was named, lest I should build upon another man's foundation" (Romans 15:20). Some overriding concern led him to abandon this policy and teach the gospel in a city where it was already established.

He may also have been willing to teach the gospel where others had already brought it to prove that gentile Christians did stand firm in the faith and that they did not pervert the gospel as some had supposed. The Roman saints, many of whom were Gentiles, could aid him in the defense of his ministry he would make to the rigorists in Jerusalem. The Pauline churches were divided and were therefore not as helpful in the argument that gentile Christian branches of the church were stable. Rome, however, seemed to be the one gentile city that Paul could draw attention to as exemplary, with the added benefit that he had not established it; therefore he could show that others had had success in gentile regions. There may have been some positive examples from his own missionary travels, and it seems that Paul used the financial generosity of the members to support his claims.

The Collection for the Poor in Jerusalem

As early as the Jerusalem conference, the leaders of the church had asked the saints from the Mediterranean region to send financial support to Jerusalem on behalf of the poor there. Frequent droughts and harsh conditions combined to create a severe famine in Judea during the reign of the emperor Claudius (A.D. 41–54).

Both Luke and Josephus include reports of the conditions. "And in these days came prophets from Jerusalem unto Antioch. And there stood up one of them named Agabus, and signified by the Spirit that there should be great dearth throughout all the world: which came to pass in the days of Claudius Caesar" (Acts 11:27–28).

The exact date of the famine cannot be ascertained, but it does appear to have happened in the early part of Claudius's reign, perhaps as early as A.D. 44. Whether the collection for the poor was intended as part of the relief effort for this famine or a second famine later in Claudius's reign is unknown. However, it is likely that the suffering in Judea continued for several years, and so Paul's activities in his final mission can be linked with the famine in the early years of Claudius's reign.

The Mediterranean missionary journeys of Paul became, in part, a welfare trip to gather money to aid in the relief of the Judean saints. Some of the branches gave generously, and Paul brought the funds to the church leaders at the conclusion of his final missionary journey. It is likely that other regions of the church contributed to the collection for the poor, but only Luke and Paul make specific mention of it in their writings.

Paul was eager to lend assistance to the poor, saying, "they would that we should remember the poor; the same which I also was forward to do" (Galatians 2:10). Paul made particular mention of the donation given by the saints of Macedonia (Philippi and Thessalonica), saying, "I bear record, yea, and beyond their power they were willing of themselves; praying us with much intreaty that we would receive the gift, and take upon us the fellowship of the ministering to the saints" (2 Corinthians 8:3–4). He also commended the saints in Achaia who were "ready a year ago" (2 Corinthians 9:2). Some of Paul's wording in speaking of the collection suggests that it was not as much as he had hoped or perhaps as much as the leaders of the church had anticipated. Paul used the occasion to remind them of the doctrine of equality, penning also the phrase, "God loveth a cheerful giver" (2 Corinthians 9:7).

By the time Paul had gathered sufficient funds to carry back with him to Jerusalem, there were very few of the original church leaders there to receive him. Whether this was a significant issue is not stated in the sources. According to Luke's report, the delivery of the collection came many years after the initial request, and his report of it may signal an underlying tension on how long the fund-raising took. Whatever the case, Paul brought the collection back to Jerusalem as he had promised, a journey that ultimately led him to his death.

Many of the saints along the way tried to convince Paul that a return to Jerusalem was suicide, but he had promised that he would bring the generous offerings of the saints to Judea. His determination reveals a profound sense of duty, one that overrode any concerns for long-term physical well-being. At the conclusion of his epistle to the Romans, he wondered whether the offering of the gentile saints would be acceptable, "and that my service which I have for Jerusalem may be accepted of the saints" (Romans 15:31).

Anti-Paul Sentiments in Rome

Word of Paul's teachings had reached the ears of the Roman saints, and some of them had perverted his words to say, "And not rather, (as we be slanderously reported, and as some affirm that we say,) Let us do evil, that good may come?" (Romans 3:8). This report was probably a widely circulated slander of Paul's teachings and may not have originated in Rome. The concern with Paul's teachings was that they would lead to wholesale abandonment of obedience to the law of Moses as well as the formation of law-free or lawless Christianity. Paul, who came to represent gentile Christians throughout the empire, often became the focus of such attacks.

The brand of Christianity that is associated with Paul is often entitled Libertine Christianity. According to Paul's detractors, his teachings led to the belief that acts of sin provided God the opportunity to forgive man and allow grace into the world; therefore such sins were in reality an act of goodness. If God forgives us for every sin, then the more that we sin the more that God will forgive us and the more grace and mercy will be in the world. Quoting the distorted teachings of his opponents, he complained, "What shall we say then? Shall we continue in sin, that grace may abound?" (Romans 6:1).

This counter to Paul's teachings was a later development in the attack against the gentile mission. Earlier the attack had centered on concerns over whether Paul's teachings encouraged disobedience to the law of Moses and to what extent Gentiles would still be required to observe its statutes. Finding out that this method of attack had proven successful in the east (Corinth) but not in the west (Rome), Paul's opponents developed new arguments that would effectively undermine the gentile mission by demonstrating the logical consequences of teaching the gospel unyoked from the law. Without the restraint of the law, Christianity would run wild—a conclusion utterly lacking faith in the power of Jesus Christ to save.

The differing views of salvation that existed among early members of the church perpetuated such problems. According to some, the law of Moses was God's law of salvation and therefore Christ's teachings were a passageway to greater obedience to the law. Their claim that the law of Moses was not done away with was valid to an extent, but rather than the law becoming a stepping-stone, the law became the way, the truth, and the life, while Jesus became the messenger leading mankind to that law. Any concessions in obedience to the law of Moses were, therefore, a corruption of God's law, obscuring the pathway to salvation.

Other Christians felt that the accumulation of good deeds would be weighed against bad deeds, with the tipping of the scale as the determining factor for salvation. Each act of obedience to the law earned a drop of oil for the lamp, while sins took that oil away. Christians were divided over whether goodness was measured against the standard of the law of Moses (Jews) or the gospel of Jesus Christ (Gentiles). This belief system quickly developed into a higher law versus the lower law dichotomy, with each side claiming the authority of the higher law.

As Paul neared the end of his life, he began to teach salvation in yet another way. He began to express salvation in terms of throwing oneself into the arms of God's mercy, begging for God's mercy to satisfy the demands of justice. For Paul, this perspective on salvation was engendered from a life of strict, and later humble, obedience, but it also reflects a changed attitude in one who had earlier thought himself blameless. In his epistle to the Romans, Paul came to the conclusion that only mercy could save in the face of an unbending law of justice.

Another form of Christianity, which was beginning to

develop in some branches of the church in the east, taught that mankind was possessed of a divine spark and that Christ came to awaken that spark within each person. The spark, variously called the spirit or soul of man, became the guiding light to salvation. Radical adherents to this belief would later reject Christ, arguing that Christ was only another example of someone who was saved, but that mankind saved himself through the recognition of and development of the spirit. Paul's final letters to the Ephesians, Colossians, Titus, and Timothy were a response to this convoluted version of Christianity.

In all of these approaches to the gospel there is a thread of truth and light, and the apostles certainly attempted to stem the pervasive effects of such heretical doctrines, but the doctrinal apostasy was already in its beginning stages.

Grace versus Works

Paul now resorted to an argument that he had been developing for his entire lifetime. He had grown up measuring his righteousness against the demands of the law, and in doing so he found himself blameless, clean, and complete. After his conversion to Christianity, he found a new standard, the gospel of Jesus Christ, a standard of perfection against which he fell short. The perfection of Christ, a divinely planned standard, was unobtainable through human means. When measured against this new standard, Paul, as all others do, fell short, and he began to search out the mercy of Christ. The epistle to the Romans represents Paul's most eloquent statement on salvation by grace, the culmination of a lifelong pursuit of perfection.

In Philippians Paul had taught that the law had become dead to him: "I count all things but loss for the excellency of the knowledge of Christ Jesus my Lord: for whom I have suffered the loss of all things, and do count them but dung, that I may win Christ" (Philippians 3:8). Later, in 2 Corinthians, he taught that the law kills: "Now the Lord is that Spirit: and where the

Spirit of the Lord is, there is liberty" (2 Corinthians 3:17). By the time he had written his epistle to the Romans he would state, "Therefore we conclude that a man is justified by faith without the deeds of the law" (Romans 3:28). In a more theologically precise passage Paul taught, "And if [salvation is] by grace, then is it no more of works: otherwise grace is no more grace. But if it be of works, then is it no more grace: otherwise work is no more work" (Romans 11:6).

Unfortunately, it is commonly presupposed that belief in salvation by grace leads to lawlessness and disobedience, but as Paul's life teaches us, those who believe in salvation by grace often work harder than anybody else. Paul never understood grace as a pathway to indolence, but rather that mercy was granted in recognition of belief: "If thou shalt confess with thy mouth the Lord Jesus, and shalt believe in thine heart that God hath raised him from the dead, thou shalt be saved" (Romans 10:9). Paul's position makes it possible to differentiate works done in faith from those done without faith, rather than to abolish the need for work. The difference between the old and the new covenants is not the nature of the work, but the center of belief. Both Jews and Gentiles worked in God's name, but faith in Christ would become the determining factor in the final judgment.

It would have been a terrible tragedy for Paul's teachings to have inspired a Christianity devoid of work and of faith-inspired acts. The very purpose for which he wrote the epistle was to gain the support of a gentile branch that had demonstrated good works throughout the world (Romans 1:8). Their obedience and exemplary conduct would aid Paul in his fight against those who felt that his teachings led to lawlessness. Why then would he provide them the doctrinal foundation that would eventually lead them to the belief that works were unnecessary for salvation? The thought probably never occurred to Paul and others who tried to live their lives in emulation of Jesus Christ.

Living a Christ-centered life meant doing the things that Jesus did, which was to give one's heart, mind, soul, and time to the spreading of the gospel. Paul had done exactly that. He left behind his ancestral religion, his hometown, and his employment in order to teach the gospel to the nations. As far as we know, he never held a job for more than a few months, he never again owned a home, he suffered tremendously while teaching the gospel, he carried all of his possessions with him, and he died in the service of the Lord. No one would ever accuse him of not working toward salvation, but he would teach that he never earned it, but rather was granted it as a gift.

MILETUS

The city of Miletus lies about twenty-five miles south of Ephesus, and as Paul traveled toward Jerusalem he stopped there rather than in Ephesus, where he was well known. Upon his arrival in "Miletus, he sent to Ephesus, and called the elders of the church. And when they were come to him, he said unto them, Ye know, from the first day that I came into Asia, after what manner I have been with you at all seasons" (Acts 20:17–18). He wanted to know about the saints in Ephesus but he did not feel comfortable traveling there himself. His report to the Romans reflects a similar sentiment: "But now having no more place in these parts" (Romans 15:23), as Judea, Syria, Galatia, Macedonia, and Greece were all closed to him.

Branches of the church continued to exist in the cities where he had founded them and in those cities where he had taught the gospel to already formed groups. Paul's departure did not signal the end of these branches, but he was now an unwelcome visitor, and having no home himself he decided to head in a new direction. Priscilla and Aquila may have been one of the main reasons that Paul intended to travel to Rome. They had left Rome after Claudius had expelled them from the capital city, but they were now permitted to return. They were trusted friends and could offer Paul lodging and employment in the city, making a visit to the city more palatable.

A CHANGE IN OUTLOOK

Luke records that shortly after his meeting with the elders from Ephesus, Paul's outlook regarding his own safety changed dramatically. Their report about continued opposition to his teachings may have caused him concern, but, as Luke told the story, Paul said, "I go bound in the spirit unto Jerusalem, not knowing the things that shall befall me there: Save that the Holy Ghost witnesseth in every city, saying that bonds and afflictions abide [await] me" (Acts 20:22–23).

A similar thought expressed by Paul to the Romans may provide the clue to his changed outlook: "And that, knowing the time, that now it is high time to awake out of sleep: *for now is our salvation nearer than when we believed.* The night is far spent, the day is at hand: let us therefore cast off the works of darkness, and let us put on the armour of light" (Romans 13:11–12; emphasis added). His reference that salvation is nearer now than it was upon his conversion is one that was informed by a lifetime of struggles and experiences. His pre-Christian attitude of blamelessness gave way to a hope in Christ, which had become for Paul an anchor to the soul. During this time in his life his hope gave way to a sure knowledge of salvation, and Paul literally began to look forward to his return to be with the Lord. The Lord had visited Paul; he now hoped to visit the Lord.

A profound sense of comfort and of spiritual stability pervaded the apostle's thoughts during this time of his life. When confronted with a spiritual assurance of his own demise, Paul responded: "None of these things move me, neither count I my life dear unto myself, so that I might finish my course with joy, and the ministry, which I have received of the Lord Jesus, to testify the gospel of the grace of God. . . . I know that ye all . . . shall see my face no more. . . . I am pure from the blood of all men" (Acts 20:24–26). His final statement is remarkably similar to the Prophet Joseph Smith's statement as he was led away to Carthage, from where he sensed he would not return. "I am going like a lamb to the slaughter; but I am calm as a summer's morning; I have a conscience void of offense towards God, and towards all men. I shall die innocent, and it shall yet be said of me—he was murdered in cold blood" (D&C 135:4). The Prophet may even have had Paul's statements to the elders of Ephesus in the back of his mind when he made that famous declaration.

Like the Prophet Joseph Smith, Paul's statement was likely informed through a direct revelation on the matter. The Lord covenanted with Joseph, saying, "For I am the Lord thy God, and will be with thee even unto the end of the world, and through all eternity; for verily I seal upon you your exaltation, and prepare a throne for you in the kingdom of my Father, with Abraham your father. Behold, I have seen your sacrifices, and will forgive all your sins; I have seen your sacrifices in obedience to that which I have told you" (D&C 132:49–50). For Paul, his experience in Ephesus seems to have provided the final adjustment to his character, the final hardening of the precious metal of his soul. For the Prophet Joseph Smith, Liberty Jail seems to have offered a similar adjustment in character, and although both were profoundly righteous before and after, their experiences in tribulation refined their souls.

PAUL PREDICTS AN APOSTASY

Early Pauline statements on the Second Coming include the personal pronoun *we* when speaking of those who will be there to greet the Lord. During the middle part of his ministry, Paul began to speak of those who would die, while others would still be alive. At the end of his life Paul was aware that he would not be alive, but that others would welcome the Lord at His coming. In his final statements to the elders of Ephesus, he taught them, "For I know this, that after my departing shall grievous wolves enter in among you, not sparing the flock. Also of your own selves shall men arise, speaking perverse things, to draw away disciples after them. Therefore watch, and remember, that by the space of three years I ceased not to warn every one night and day with tears" (Acts 20:29–31). The effects of apostasy would spread through the branches as a wildfire. Paul had already seen the doctrinal apostasy that had plagued the branches, but the apostasy of ordinances and authority was yet to come.

His dour prophecy broke the hearts of those who came to meet him in Miletus. "And they all wept sore, and fell on Paul's neck, and kissed him. Sorrowing most of all for the words which he spake, that they should see his face no more" (Acts 20:37–38). In that Spirit-filled room, Paul testified that he would not return, and their tears upon hearing his prophecy revealed that the Spirit confirmed the prophecy in their hearts.

JERUSALEM

From Miletus, Paul and his fellow missionaries boarded a cargo ship bound for Tyre. In the city they located other Christians "who said to Paul through the Spirit, that he should not go up to Jerusalem" (Acts 21:4). Their stay in Tyre was short-lived, and Paul gathered the saints together on the shores of the Mediterranean and there offered a prayer. Luke records that the members came out to meet him, "with wives and children" (Acts 21:5), suggesting that Paul may have given them an apostolic blessing. Unlike his previous travels, each branch of the church seems to have been aware that this would be their last opportunity to see Paul. He went to great lengths to report how the members loved him, but at the same time he was careful to report that these warm receptions took place in cities where he had not taught the gospel ("No prophet is accepted in his own country" [Luke 4:24]).

Together with his small missionary party, Paul boarded a ship headed toward Caesarea, where he was welcomed into the home of Philip the evangelist, one of the seven who was called with Stephen to administer relief to the widows in Jerusalem (Acts 21:8). About fifty miles from Jerusalem, Caesarea functioned as a port for the region of Judea, and Paul and his companions intended to travel on foot to the capital city.

A Christian prophet named Agabus made the journey to Caesarea to greet the missionaries and met them while they were staying in the home of Philip: "And when he was come unto us, he took Paul's girdle, and bound his own hands and feet, and said, Thus saith the Holy Ghost, So shall the Jews at Jerusalem bind the man that owneth this girdle, and shall deliver him into the hands of the Gentiles. And when we heard these things, both we, and they of that place, besought him not to go up to Jerusalem" (Acts 21:11–12).

This prophetic glimpse into Paul's future served as both a confirmation of what the apostle had already learned through the Spirit and as a test of his resolve. He already knew that he would face trials in Jerusalem, including arrest and imprisonment, but nothing he had said or experienced previously caused those closest to him to oppose his trip to Jerusalem (Acts 20:22–27). Now, through the prophet Agabus, his friends had a second witness to Paul's promptings.

Paul, who never mentions any close family members or relatives, had found support through a network of friends and close missionary companions, many of whom had been with him since his early missionary work in Asia. These friends and companions became Paul's family. Like the Prophet Joseph Smith's family, who watched him be taken away to certain death, Paul's companions presented the last significant obstacle to overcome. Facing trial alone is a daunting task and creates its own peculiar set of challenges. Private trials can lead to doubt, the loss of hope, feelings of despair, and at times depression; however, some trials are more public. Usually the prophets face very public trials, which are divinely orchestrated efforts that eventually establish an example of faith for future generations.

Paul's final trial was accepting his own death even after he learned that so many still loved him. He had already decided that he could willingly accept his own death. He had been forced out of nearly all the cities where he had taught the gospel, but now he found that he was also profoundly loved. Not only did those closest to him love him, but members from nearby branches came out to see him and weep at his departure. He had previously reflected, "if I live in the flesh, this is the fruit of my labour: yet what I shall choose I wot not. For I am in a strait betwixt two, having a desire to depart, and to be with Christ; which is far better: Nevertheless to abide in the flesh is more needful for you" (Philippians 1:22–24).

Paul, who had no known family support, now faced the most daunting challenge of all, leaving behind his new family. Dearly beloved and solid in the testimony that he would never see some of his friends again in the flesh, Paul set off toward Jerusalem. "What mean ye to weep and to break mine heart? for I am ready not to be bound only, but also to die at Jerusalem for the name of the Lord Jesus. And when he would not be persuaded, we ceased, saying, The will of the Lord be done" (Acts 21:13–14).

Chapter 8

PAUL ARRIVES IN JERUSALEM

"Paul, as Peter, had his hours of discouragement. Pride sometimes perturbed him, and conformity to church authority was occasionally difficult. He, too, was mobbed, beaten, and imprisoned, put in stocks in a dungeon, but the heavenly vision of the risen Lord ever guided his footsteps."
—David O. McKay

Luke records that Paul and his missionary companions were received with gladness in Jerusalem and that a superficial euphoria permeated the atmosphere when they arrived. He was greeted by James, Jesus' younger brother, who gave Paul an opportunity to report on his mission to the Gentiles. Luke notes: "Paul went in with us unto James; *and all the elders were present.* And when he had saluted them, he declared particularly what things God had wrought among the Gentiles by his ministry. And when they heard it, they glorified the Lord, and said unto him, Thou seest, brother, how many thousands of Jews there are which believe; and they are all zealous of the law" (Acts 21:18–20; emphasis added). Their apparently favorable reaction was in essence a warning, and although it may initially seem positive in some regards, he was counseled to proceed with caution in making his report known among the saints in Jerusalem.

Who Luke intended with the designation "elders" in this account is unclear, because, after hearing Paul's report, James warned him, saying, "*they are informed of thee,* that thou teachest all the Jews which are among the Gentiles to forsake Moses, saying that they ought not to circumcise their children, neither to walk after the customs" (Acts 21:21; emphasis added). Having delivered his missionary report, Paul was told that the locals had been "informed" about him before his arrival and that they had great concerns about his teachings. With one foot in Judaism and one foot in Christianity, these members were not concerned that Paul had taught the gospel to Gentiles, but that while he was teaching the gospel to Gentiles he had encouraged Jews to disobey portions of the law of Moses. As proof they could have cited Romans, in which Paul taught, "For he is not a Jew, which is one outwardly; neither is that circumcision, which is outward in the flesh: But he is a Jew, which is one inwardly; and circumcision is that of the heart, in the spirit, and not in the letter; whose praise is not of men, but of God" (Romans 2:28–29).

The early church, particularly the Jerusalem branches, seemed to have faced a cyclical rebirth of this issue, each decade recasting it to express their own particular concerns. An earlier generation had feared that any mission to the Gentiles would ultimately lead to the corruption of the law by allowing Gentiles to live it in an abbreviated form, causing Jews who were aware of this concession to slacken in their obedience when they saw the example set by the Gentiles.

This new formulation of the issue shows that the concern was that in teaching Gentiles to follow the directions of the Jerusalem council, Paul was also teaching Jews to break the commandment of circumcision. The council had decided that

Gentiles were not obligated to be circumcised, but they feared Paul was extending this exception to Jewish members of the church also. Encouraging such a practice would have been contrary to the directions of the council, and Paul would have been found in opposition to official church policy. The evidence that they had against him, however, was apparently derived from written sources and not actual examples, and therefore the issue was expressed as a concern rather than as an accusation.

THE TEST

These elders had planned their strategy well, and proposed to Paul that he prove his devotion to the law through the fulfillment of a Nazarite vow. They assured him, "Do therefore this that we say to thee: We have four men which have a vow on them; Them take, and purify thyself with them, and be at charges with them, that they may shave their heads: and all may know that those things, whereof they were informed concerning thee, are nothing; but that thou thyself also walkest orderly, and keepest the law. As touching the Gentiles which believe, we have written and concluded that they observe no such thing, save only that they keep themselves from things offered to idols, and from blood, and from [things] strangled, and from fornication" (Acts 21:23–25). Their counsel was in essence a reaffirmation of the decision made by the Jerusalem council, an intentional reference by Luke to indicate that the elders were connected with the rigorists who made demands during the first Jerusalem council.

They had predetermined that Paul could prove his faithfulness if he would take four other men with him to the temple and there complete a Nazarite vow. They also asked that Paul pay for all of the sacrifices as proof of his sincerity. This plan, according to Luke, was carried out under the direction of these same elders who had heard his initial report. The test, however, proved to be a trap, and Paul was immediately arrested in his attempt to placate the rigorists in Jerusalem.

Luke reports that the elders presented the four men to Paul and that he had not known them prior to coming to Jerusalem. At the conclusion of the seven-day vow, some Jews of Asia pressed for his arrest because he had brought an uncircumcised Greek into the temple. Because circumcision is not an externally identifiable sign, the plan to send Trophimus into the temple must have been prearranged so that they would have definitive evidence against Paul for polluting the house of the Lord (Acts 21:27–29).

Trophimus's exact whereabouts during the arrest are difficult to pinpoint, and the story can be read in two different ways. Trophimus of Ephesus first appears in Acts in the previous chapter (Acts 20:4) when he was sent with other missionaries from Macedonia to Troas to wait for the apostle's arrival. Only one other mention is made of Trophimus, who was left at Miletus sick while Paul traveled to Rome and is presumably the same person mentioned in Acts (2 Timothy 4:20). Whether the person named Trophimus in the temple story is the same as that mentioned as a missionary companion of Paul is impossible to know. Luke also seems to have been unaware of the exact role of Trophimus in Paul's arrest. Interestingly, in Paul's public defense of his actions and ministry before the Jerusalem mob that had him arrested, he made no mention of Trophimus's presence in the temple or the Greeks that he had supposedly brought into the temple. In his mind, the issue was that he had taught the gospel to Gentiles and that the Lord told him the Jews would not believe (Acts 22:18–22).

Luke relates that some of Paul's opponents had seen him in the city with Trophimus and "they supposed that Paul had brought [him] into the temple," which hardly seems significant enough impetus to incite a riot and have Paul arrested on the spot (Acts 21:29). In another verse, Luke relates that the mob became excited when they learned that Paul had taken Greeks into the temple. If the mobs had seen Paul with Trophimus in the city and later in the temple, then there may have been sufficient reason to call for his arrest. Luke records, however, that several Greeks were brought into the temple, an almost certain reference to the men who entered the temple with Paul to complete their Nazarite vow. Why they waited until the end of the seven-day period is also unclear; they could easily have raised the same concern at the beginning, although the setup would have been more immediately transparent.

Historically, the most plausible solution seems to be that Paul was accused of taking uncircumcised Greeks with him into the temple (the same men who were introduced to him during the elders' plan for Paul to prove his faithfulness) and that Trophimus, who probably never entered the temple, may have been implicated in the plot to divert attention away from the four who did enter the temple with Paul. The whole account reeks of subtlety and intrigue, and Luke's elders seem to have been in the middle of the plot. Inspired priesthood leaders do not develop plans whereby other church leaders can prove their sincerity and faithfulness. James, who was presiding over a branch beset with apostasy, likely represented the minority of the branch, who sustained Paul as an apostle and missionary of the Lord Jesus Christ. Paul, on his part, was convinced prior to his arrival in Jerusalem that things would go poorly there and therefore was willing to submit to the whims of the local Jewish leaders as he had done in other instances when they had administered the thirty-nine lashes.

James may have suffered the consequences of his support of Paul, and shortly thereafter (in A.D. 62) he was martyred in Jerusalem by a local mob. The fourth-century historian Eusebius made a similar connection when he reported, "When Paul appealed to Caesar and was sent to Rome by Festus, the Jews were disappointed of the hope in which they had devised their plot against him and turned their attention to James the Lord's brother, who had been elected by the apostles to the episcopal throne at Jerusalem. This is the crime that they committed against him. They brought him into their midst and in the presence of the whole populace demanded a denial of his belief in Christ. But . . . declaring that our Saviour and Lord, Jesus, was the Son of God, they could not endure his testimony any longer. . . . So they killed him" (*Church History*, 2.23). The fallout from Paul's arrest and escape from death extended to James, revealing that James remained devoted to Christianity even though corrupt elders surrounded him.

PAUL'S ROMAN CITIZENSHIP

Had Paul not been a Roman citizen, he likely would have died at the hands of the Jerusalem mobs. Fortunately for Paul, someone in the crowd alerted the Roman garrison in Jerusalem that the city was in a state of near chaos, so that soldiers came quickly and arrested Paul, thus preserving his life. Paul was also able to avoid being "examined by scourging" because, as a Roman citizen, he had the right to a trial before any punishment was meted out.

Under arrest and bound for prison, Paul was led away to the "castle," or more literally to the barracks of the Roman soldiers stationed in Jerusalem, where he would be safe from the mobs (Acts 22:24). Luke, who was probably not present for the proceedings, makes his report in broad strokes, filling in few of the details while leaving a multitude of unanswered questions.

According to his report, the local magistrate or chief captain of the Roman troops in Jerusalem, Claudius Lysias, called for a general meeting of members of the Sanhedrin (Acts 23:26). It is unlikely that a Roman official could call for a meeting of the Sanhedrin or that they would gather at his command. From Luke's account, it also seems that Claudius Lysias was in attendance at the meeting, indicating that the Sanhedrin had permitted a Roman official to defile their sanctuary. Historically, the local Roman chief captain would use local Jews as witnesses in his attempt to discover what Paul was accused of, and in this instance the majority of those local Jews turned out to have connections with the Sanhedrin. Leaving Paul in the Sanhedrin would place him in unnecessary danger, and as a Roman citizen Paul had certain rights to a fair and safe trial.

Luke reports that this fact-finding expedition evolved into a doctrinal dispute between Pharisees and Sadducees concerning the validity of the resurrection. If the gathered officials were so narrowly focused and united on the point of condemning Paul, then it is strange that they were so easily sidetracked. It may be, however, that one faction of the Sanhedrin (Pharisees) had sympathy for Paul, while the other faction (Sadducees), whose more rigid beliefs demanded that he die, were unwavering in their condemnation. Even during Jesus' ministry, there was a division along Pharisaic and Sadduceean lines in the Sanhedrin regarding Christ and his teachings (John 7:45–53).

Because of this initial setback in their plans to have Paul condemned to death, a small group of rigorist Jews entered into a plot to kill Paul the next day when he was returned to the council of Jews for further questioning. A nephew of Paul's discovered the plot, and when it was made known to the chief captain Paul was taken to Caesarea under heavy guard (Acts 23:14–24).

Antonius Felix (A.D. 52–59/60), or simply Felix as Luke referred to him, is generally perceived as a governor who faced severe political corruption during his tenure. Josephus reports that Judea was rife with insurrection and antigovernment activity under Felix and that he became involved in a war against an organized group of bandits. One particular report repeats the common sentiment that Felix was either involved in the corruption prevalent in Jerusalem or that he was not beyond accepting bribes and extending favors: "Felix also bore an ill will to Jonathan, the high priest, because he frequently gave him admonitions about governing the Jewish affairs better than he did. . . . So Felix contrived a method whereby he might get rid of him, now he was become so continually troublesome to him" (Josephus, *Antiquities,* 20.8.5). Luke records a similar sentiment about Felix, saying, "He hoped also that money should have been given him of Paul, that he might loose him: wherefore he sent for him the oftener, and communed with him" (Acts 24:26).

Paul's stay in Caesarea was likely relatively peaceful and uneventful. While under house arrest, he would have had the privilege of accepting visitors, writing letters, and sending missionaries out to visit the branches where he had served as a missionary. His time in Caesarea was extended as Felix attempted to gather information about Paul and to make an accounting of the charges made against him by his countrymen. The plot to arrest Paul seems to have fallen apart during this time because Ananias, the high priest, was unable to bring any of the original witnesses with him to Caesarea to confront Paul; instead he was forced to rely on a professional orator to express his case. Because there was no opportunity to confront his accusers, Paul should have been free to move on, the charges against him being dismissed. Felix, however, willing to placate the Jews but careful not to treat Paul unjustly, continued to hold him over for trial.

COLOSSIANS AND EPHESIANS

Faced with a lengthy house arrest, Paul took the opportunity to write to some of the areas where he had taught the gospel. In these two epistles—Colossians and Ephesians—Paul wrote to communities that did not seem to know him. "For I would that ye knew what great conflict I have for you, and for them at Laodicea, and for as many as have not seen my face in the flesh" (Colossians 2:1). Paul also did not seem to be known to the recipients of the letter now entitled Ephesians: "Wherefore I also, after I heard of your faith in the Lord Jesus, and love unto all the saints" (Ephesians 1:15). Given that Luke records a two-year stay in Ephesus (Acts 19:10), it is strange that Paul does not seem to know them when he wrote to them after his visit there.

The answers to these historical difficulties come from several different sources. Both communities—Ephesus and Colossae—were cities in Asia, the very region from which the elders came who accused Paul of polluting the temple (Acts 21:27). It was not unlike Paul to directly confront his accusers, or in this case send two positive letters to the saints thanking them for their faith and support even though some of their own had turned against him. The second piece of evidence comes from the earliest manuscripts of the New Testament, which do not contain the title "Ephesus." The letter that we now associate with Ephesus was likely never written to that city specifically, but to the region of Asia, where it was intended as a circular letter to those branches who remained faithful and from whom Paul hoped to garner support. The most famous of the cities, Ephesus, eventually lent its name to the epistle, but in so doing confused the historical setting from which it originated. Around A.D. 60–61 Paul began writing letters in defense of his mission and what he had taught the Gentiles. Ephesians and Colossians form part of a trio, together with the lost letter to Laodicea. The surviving two epistles offer a plea for support and a call for continued faith even though some of their own had departed from the faith (Colossians 4:16).

From these two epistles, we learn that Timothy was with Paul as were Aristarchus, Mark, Jesus Justus, Epaphras, Luke, Demas, and Tychicus (Ephesians 6:21; Colossians 4:10–12, 14). Tychicus carried both letters to their destinations, where he also gave an oral report of Paul's situation in Caesarea (Ephesians 6:21; Colossians 4:7). His presence in the two letters links them together and suggests that both were written at nearly the same time.

The letters also share a considerable amount of new vocabulary, compared with the earlier epistles, causing some to discount these letters as genuine epistles of Paul. Luke may have inadvertently provided an explanation for this, however, for he records that Paul may have been blind, or nearly blind at this time. His earlier thorn in the flesh appears to have grown worse in the final years of his missions and by the time he arrived in Jerusalem (Acts 23:3–5, where he seems to be unable to recognize the high priest). His blindness would have forced him to use a scribe to write his letters, and Ephesians and Colossians, which have much in common, were likely written by the same scribe during the imprisonment at Caesarea. In both epistles Paul is relatively optimistic that the charges against him would be overturned, a position that is likely a response to the fact that Ananias was unable to produce any credible witnesses.

The core issue of these two epistles was the division resulting between those who claimed to have greater spiritual knowledge and those who had been disparaged as having insufficient knowledge. In reality, the issue could be described as a conflict between a higher law and a lower law. When any group within the church begins to feel that it has not only identified the higher law but also now lives it, they will eventually marginalize and disparage those who do not live such higher-law standards. The origin of this division need not be the introduction of philosophical concepts into the gospel message, but rather may stem from the Jerusalem council's decision directing one group of members (Jews) to live all of the law of Moses, while others (Gentiles) were only required to live a portion of it.

Paul's language reflects such a division and answers it in a new way. Rather than attack the problem by attacking the rigorist faction, Paul presented a doctrinal assault on the faulty presuppositions of those who claimed to have higher knowledge. Paul denigrates those who teach "philosophy" and who have been inspired by the "rudiments of the world" but not by God or Christ (Colossians 2:8). He also taught that their positions were inspired by their observation of festivals and diets (Colossians 2:16) and by their claim to live an ascetic lifestyle, depriving themselves of worldly pleasures in order to prove their spirituality (Colossians 2:20–22). Moreover, Paul teaches, "Let no man beguile you of your reward in a voluntary humility and worshipping of angels, intruding into those things which he hath not seen, vainly puffed up by his fleshly mind" (Colossians 2:18).

When viewed collectively, Paul's statements reveal a strand of Christianity that held to the principle that spiritual maturity and knowledge are the result of physical asceticism (diets and fasting) while focusing on unique doctrinal concepts, which he terms "philosophy," which is not unlike the modern world where knowledge and external Christianity are often used to define spirituality. When viewed in isolation, spirituality defined by external manifestations leads only to pride, to division, and to higher law Christianity. Instead, Paul advocated, "put on charity, which is the bond of perfectness. And let the peace of God rule in your hearts, to the which also ye are called in one body; and be ye thankful. Let the word of Christ dwell in you richly in all wisdom; teaching and admonishing one another in psalms and hymns and spiritual songs, singing with grace in your hearts to the Lord" (Colossians 3:14–16). Paul knew that internal conversion would lead to positive external Christian works, while external religion may simply be the manifestation of skin-deep conversion.

FESTUS REPLACES FELIX

After two years, Porcius Festus replaced Felix as governor of Judea. He served for a period of about two years (A.D. 59/60–62), placing Paul's imprisonment in Caesarea between Pentecost (May) A.D. 58 through spring A.D. 60. Roman governors usually arrived at their new cities in late spring, and Luke's account would confirm that Festus arrived in Caesarea around Pentecost in about A.D. 60; roughly two years after Paul had arrived in Jerusalem with the collection for the poor. Festus, who seems to have been more evenhanded than his predecessor Felix, replaced the latter because of intrigue and corruption in his government. Nero, an able administrator in his early years, may also have been concerned with the continued problem of banditry and lawlessness prevalent in Judea (Josephus, *Antiquities*, 20.8.9–10). Nothing is known of Festus's character other than that he immediately went about wrapping up the older cases left behind after Felix's departure for Rome.

By now, Paul had become somewhat of a fixture in Felix's court, and when Festus replaced Felix he inherited the legal quagmire of hearing Paul's case. Felix, whose relationship with Jonathan the high priest became increasingly strained, appears to have rejected any claims made by him. Rather, he preferred to work with Ananias, who held the office of high priest from A.D. 47 through A.D. 55 and still wielded some influence with the Judean governors. Jonathan would have had greater influence in Judean politics than Ananias, but Felix did not get along with him. This bad relationship was likely opportune for Paul, who was not forced to suffer the unjust punishment of a legal decision brokered as a favor to the high priest. Instead,

Felix seems to have given only Ananias an opportunity to present evidence. Some ancient manuscripts of Acts add that Ananias made a special plea to Felix based on the fact that the Jews had tried to judge Paul according to their own laws, but the chief captain (Claudius Lysias) took Paul away from them. If Felix would remand Paul to their jurisdiction, Ananias would readily hear and judge the case, a plea that Felix did not honor.

When Festus received the case, he immediately reinterviewed the witnesses against Paul, trying to determine the nature of the charge against him. Felix would have left him information concerning the case, but obviously left nothing of substance whereby Festus could bring formal charges. Instead, Festus had to seek out the high priest (Jonathan) to ascertain what evidence there was against Paul. In an action that appears to be evenhanded, Festus would not accept Jonathan's plea to have Paul brought to Jerusalem for trial, but instead required the high priest to bring any witnesses against Paul to Caesarea. Upon closer inspection, the case against Paul fell apart a second time.

To break the stalemate in the case, Festus proposed to Paul that he be sent back to Jerusalem for trial. Whether Festus really intended to send Paul there for trial is uncertain, but in an act of desperation the ruse succeeded and Paul requested that he be sent to Rome for trial rather than face unjust punishment and certain death in Jerusalem.

Festus did not seem entirely satisfied with Paul's request to have a hearing from the emperor, and therefore he sought to settle the issue through the question of jurisdiction, which was certainly a dispute in the matter of Paul. Paul, who was a citizen of Tarsus (Acts 22:3), could certainly be brought to trial in Judea for crimes committed in that region. If, however, he could transfer the case to Herod Agrippa I and remand Paul to that court, then he could avoid some of the political turmoil that had embroiled Felix's court. The attempt to transfer jurisdiction in the case, however, may have been based on a specious argument, and may have stemmed from the fact that Paul had family in Galilee, or that his ancestors originated from those regions.

The appeal to Herod Agrippa I, according to Luke, was made in an attempt to gather information about the charges against Paul. Luke felt that the reason Paul was sent to Agrippa was to help Festus understand the nuances of the case before him (Acts 25:26–27). Paul's defense before Agrippa would also have clarified the matter of jurisdiction in the case, determining whether it was appropriate to release Paul or whether, since it appeared to be a question of Jewish law, Herod could hear the case.

Luke concludes the account of Paul's hearing before Festus and Agrippa with the statement that Paul could have been set free had he not requested a hearing in Rome: "And when he had thus spoken, the king rose up, and the governor, and Bernice, and they that sat with them: And when they were gone aside, they talked between themselves, saying, This man doeth nothing worthy of death or of bonds. Then said Agrippa unto Festus, This man might have been set at liberty, if he had not appealed unto Caesar" (Acts 26:30–32). If Festus offered Paul his freedom, then it seems unlikely that Paul would have rejected the offer. Agrippa, however, felt that Paul should be set free, which was probably his legal opinion in the case regarding both jurisdiction and the nature of the charges. Festus, who Luke had said was using Agrippa to find out about the charges, did not accept his opinion, but rather held Paul in prison until he could be sent to Rome.

HEBREWS

Sometime after Paul became certain that he would not be released from his imprisonment in Caesarea, and possibly as late as his Roman imprisonment, he wrote a general epistle to all Jewish Christians defending the gospel of Jesus Christ from the perspective of a Jewish convert. Hebrews was likely not written as a letter, and it bears only hints of a letter format. It is also the only Pauline letter that was not written to a congregation or to an individual, but rather was written to an entire nation or people. In it Paul presents the doctrine of Christ using Jewish themes and terminology.

A quick glance at the themes of this letter reveals Paul's purpose in writing it. He begins by revealing Christ's role in creation, stating that the Creator—Jesus Christ—was the agent of the Father and therefore the God of the Old Testament. He then goes on to state that Jesus is greater than the angels of heaven (Hebrews 1:5–2:18); he is superior to Moses and Joshua (Hebrews 3:1–4:13); he is the great high priest and superior to earthly high priests (Hebrews 4:14–7:28); he received better promises for mankind (Hebrews 8:1–9:22); his sacrifice was infinite (Hebrews 9:23–10:31); and he was now the perfect example for the faithful to follow (Hebrews 12:1–13:19). The beauty of this formulation is that Christ is superior to any earthly example, particularly to the great examples of faith and law in Jewish tradition.

Perhaps the greatest exposition of this epistle can be found at the end of the fourth chapter, where Paul teaches how Jesus has provided access for us into God's grace. Annually the high priest would enter the Holy of Holies on the Day of Atonement after sprinkling the blood of sacrifice on the altar in his own behalf and in behalf of Israel. Paul recognized the power of this symbol, which taught the children of Israel that they could come into God's presence only through a mediator. They could not directly enter the Holy of Holies, but instead the high priest could enter once a year only after he had been properly cleansed.

Christ, Paul taught, had opened the way into the Holy of Holies to all. Jesus had entered into the Holy of Holies and taken up his abode rather than departing as the high priest had done. In the Holy of Holies, Christ now held court and invited all to enter into his presence and partake of his grace and mercy. Christ opened the way into the holiest place of the temple through his sufferings and temptations, and now that he had experienced the vicissitudes of humanity, he was ready to sit and judge mankind with unreserved kindness (Hebrews 4:15–16). Christ was and is the great mediator of mankind, and unlike the Mosaic high priests, he could make intercession for man not only because he had been offered as a sacrifice for their sins, but also because he had participated in their sufferings.

As a defense of his own ministry, particularly his testimony of Christ, Hebrews presents a clear picture of Paul's thoughts on the eternal role of Christ. The letter also has many unique characteristics, causing some to question Paul's authorship. Such a plea to Jews, however, would likely have been written in Aramaic and not in Greek as his other epistles, so many of the differences could be traced to issues of translation and the use of a scribe. In spite of its uniqueness, the fact that the earliest traditions link it with Paul recommends its authenticity.

TRAVEL TO ROME

Luke seems to imply that Festus sent Paul to Rome during the sailing season, which would have begun after mid-March when winds were favorable and the chances for major storms in the Mediterranean would have subsided significantly (Acts 27:1). In reality, Paul and his companions departed very late in the season, and now faced the significant threat of storms at sea.

The ship that Paul boarded headed up the Phoenician coastline, thus setting off with little difficulty. At Sidon on the northern Phoenician coast, the captain changed course and headed in the direction of Asia, following what appears to be a trade route rather than a more direct route to Rome. That Paul would have traveled on a commercial trading vessel is almost certain, and the frequent stops made along the Asian coastline make it obvious that this was the case (Acts 27:2–8). Paul traveled with a small band of soldiers who guaranteed his safety as well as his arrival in Rome.

At this stage in their journey, Luke relates that Paul and his traveling companions encountered unfavorable winds and that they tried to use the islands as cover from the wind in their journey toward Rome. The crew put in at Fair Havens, where Luke reports that they had been caught off guard by early winds. Typically the sailing season would extend from mid-March to mid-September, but according to Acts they had pushed their luck by sailing past the normal sailing season: "Now when much time was spent, and when sailing was now dangerous, because the fast was now already past" (Acts 27:9). The "fast" or Day of Atonement—the only fast in the Jewish calendar—mentioned in this passage took place near the end of September, suggesting that the ship's captain had already extended the normal sailing season by a week or two. Josephus reports that it was common in the first century to fear any sea travel after the end of September: "He also took so much pleasure there, that he abode many days with them, and would willingly have staid longer, but that the season of the year made him make haste away; for as winter was coming on, he thought it not safe to go to sea later" (*Antiquities*, 16.2.1).

Led on by the false impression of a favorable southeastern wind so late in the season, the captain of the ship again set sail and departed from Fair Havens, believing it to be a poor spot to remain in. "And because the haven was not commodius to winter in, the more part advised to depart thence also, if by any means they might attain to Phenice" (Acts 27:12), a more accommodating harbor. Paul objected to the decision to continue sailing so late in the season but not necessarily against the decision to travel to a larger and more protected harbor, and he prophesied that the ship's cargo would be lost if they endeavored to leave Fair Havens at that time of year (Acts 27:9–11). Neither the ship's captain nor the officer in charge of Paul considered his plea.

The port at Fair Havens is located along a beautiful stretch of Mediterranean coast, but its harbor is small and relatively unprotected in comparison to other major commercial harbors. The island also offered little opportunity to sell off commercial goods, such as perishable items, if that was necessary.

The trip from Fair Havens began smoothly, but the travelers soon met unfriendly weather en route to Malta. Luke reports that they encountered "a tempestuous wind, called Euroclydon" (Acts 27:14). The winds that Luke refers to are almost certainly the hot dry desert winds that scorch North Africa and are today called Sirocco. These terrible winds could shred the sails of the ship and force her into uncharted waters; therefore, the most immediate response would be to lower the sails to see if the storm would blow past them quickly. On the first day of the storm they spent their time taking down the sails, tying down the loose cargo, and attempting to secure everything that could be lost to the winds and the waves.

Luke gives the impression that the storm was horrific, and with her sails down the ship itself was still in danger of breaking apart and being pushed into a sandbar near the coast of a nearby island. With a heavy cargo and without sails, the ship would have been at the mercy of the elements. To escape the sandbar, the crew struck sail and attempted to move the ship into deeper water. They did reach deeper waters, but the ship was nearly torn apart by exposure to the winds.

On the third day of the storm the crew threw the rigging

into the sea, a sign of absolute desperation. Luke, who was unconcerned with providing precise details about the storm, is probably referring to the sails and the rigging associated with them, which had by this time been torn to shreds in the winds. Seeking to save the ship, the crew also lightened the ship by unloading the cargo into the sea and thus fulfilling Paul's prophecy. If the crew were to be saved at this point, then it would have to be without their ship, which had now been entirely disabled in the storm. They may have taken such measures because they knew land was nearby, but in gale force winds the ship could easily have been pushed a long distance from the rocks and the sandbar that they had encountered during the first two days of the storm.

Realizing how desperate their circumstances really were, the crew abandoned ship near Malta, on an island inhabited by barbarians. To the Greeks and Romans, barbarians were any society or people who spoke a language other than the widely recognized languages of the Roman empire. Anciently someone had described them as people whose speech was "bar, bar, bar." Eventually the description was used to designate any culture that spoke a foreign language and the term *bar-bar-ians* stuck. The native people of Malta were considered barbarians and the crew was surprised to see how well the people treated them.

The next event that transpired reveals Luke's reason for relating the account. In the first century, belief in divine justice and fate permeated society. Today such belief would be termed superstitious and usually disparaged as childish or ignorant. However, to utterly spurn belief in the gods, fate, and justice in Paul's day would be considered impious and atheistic. Although not immediately, the terrible storm and resulting shipwreck would have been interpreted as a sign of punishment for the criminal Paul. The proof came when the stranded sailors made a fire and a poisonous snake came out of a woodpile and bit

Paul on the hand. In that instance the people of Malta had proof that Paul, who had escaped justice momentarily, was now being punished for his actions. God would not permit him to escape justice.

In a matter of a few minutes Paul went from being perceived as a condemned criminal to being esteemed as deity. As the crew and others watched for the time when Paul should have fallen ill, they were disappointed, and they immediately changed their opinion of him. "And when the barbarians saw the venomous beast hang on his hand, they said among themselves, No doubt this man is a murderer, whom, though he hath escaped the sea, yet vengeance suffereth not to live. And he shook off the beast into the fire, and felt no harm. Howbeit they looked when he should have swollen, or fallen down dead suddenly: but after they had looked a great while, and saw no harm come to him, they changed their minds, and said that he was a god" (Acts 28:4–6). Luke's purpose in narrating the story is to show that the crew now had two definite witnesses that Paul was a prophet of God and that he had been unjustly condemned.

In narrating the final events in Paul's life, Luke moves quickly between the two witnesses of having correctly prophesied the ship's fate and surviving the snake bite, passing over the details of their travels, layovers, time spent in travel, and other important details that would indicate he was trying to write a history of Paul's life. Instead, Luke is intent on bearing testimony of the man he so deeply admired and esteemed; therefore, he labors to show that Paul was condemned unjustly and that those who were involved in his arrest and trial had sufficient testimony of that innocence.

The crew likely spent the winter months in Malta, perhaps staying from early October through mid-March when it was safe to travel again. They eventually found their way on a packet ship out of North Africa headed to Rome. During the first century, thousands of such ships would make their way from North Africa to Rome, carrying grain and other staple goods from the thriving and lush Nile River Valley to Rome, where a public grain dole had functioned since the early days of the empire.

At this point Luke seems to have lost interest in narrating the story, or at least this has been the impression that many have had about his account of Paul's final days in Rome. Numerous theories have tried to explain why Luke did not provide an account of Paul's trial in Rome or his subsequent death. In fact, the lack of information was already appreciated in the third century A.D. when an apocryphal *Acts of Paul* surfaced to explain this very period in Paul's life. This often-fanciful work should clearly be considered a work of fiction by modern standards, but it is also the earliest legendary account of Paul's death.

As Paul and his small group of guards made their way to Rome, they would have saluted the few saints who had converted to the gospel in Italy, where Peter led the missionary work. Paul certainly would have found some members there, particularly in Rome. Under guard, he would not have been permitted to stay with them for long because he had been remanded to Rome for trial.

Under the rule of Nero, Rome in the early to mid-60s was a society bursting at the seams with iniquity. Contemporary accounts reveal a dark side of Roman culture that rivals the biblical accounts of Sodom and Gomorrah. Nero, who had proven himself an able administrator in the early part of his reign, had been seized with a passion to experience all things distasteful. He had developed a peculiar taste for pomp and grandeur, and during the latter part of his reign he began prosecuting more individuals for crimes against the emperor's majesty (*maiestas*), which in modern legal terminology would be interpreted as treason. This charge was almost certainly the same charge made against Jesus at his trial before Pilate, and it could be loosely construed to include any act that diminished the power, might, and majesty of the emperor or his domains.

For Paul, who was already facing trumped-up charges from his rivals in Jerusalem and a political climate that had deteriorated into intrigue and scandal, a Roman trial before Caesar did not seem particularly beneficial. Luke brings his account of Paul's life to an end here, with the apostle having arrived safely in Rome and awaiting trial before Nero Caesar. Luke reports only that Paul spent two years in relative peace while being held over for trial. He was in a position to meet with the saints in Rome. It is not unlikely that he had the occasion to meet with Peter, who was also in Rome during the latter years of Nero's reign (A.D. 54–68).

It was during these final two years that Paul spent in Rome that he penned three personal epistles to his beloved missionary companions, both of whom had remained close to him since their early days together in Asia. These two companions—Timothy and Titus—had avoided capture in Jerusalem and were now serving faithfully as bishops in the areas of Paul's former missionary cities. Whether and when Paul wrote these epistles has been debated in the modern era, but the early church universally accepted them as Pauline. Without any direct historical information to date the epistles, debate will almost certainly continue. It seems wise to follow the early church and accept these epistles as genuine reminiscences of the apostle to two of his closest friends, even though their wording may reveal the work of a scribe or editor.

THE PASTORALS—TIMOTHY AND TITUS

The three letters, 1 and 2 Timothy and Titus, contain very little internal information about Paul's whereabouts or circumstances when they were written. All were probably written at different times in Paul's life and may not presently be placed in their historical order. Titus is mentioned as an emissary to Crete near the location of Paul's shipwreck in Acts 27:7–15. Paul mentions that he intends to winter in Nicopolis, which unfortunately does not reveal his whereabouts because several cities of that name existed in the Mediterranean region (Titus 1:5; 3:12). In 2 Timothy, Paul is in prison—probably in Rome—where he refers to a first defense (2 Timothy 4:16–17). Paul also lists several of his traveling companions, including Trophimus who was present with Paul in Jerusalem and who joined with Paul during the final months of his final mission (2 Timothy 4:9–21; Acts 21:29).

The solution to the problem would be to recognize that both Acts and Paul's letters are incomplete accounts that document only portions of Paul's life and that neither Luke nor Paul ever intended to write a complete history.

Unlike his earlier epistles, the pastoral epistles focus in part on the priesthood offices of bishop and deacon. Both Timothy and Titus appear to have been in positions where they would either be calling new bishops and deacons or were to help train those who were already serving in those capacities. Paul also treated several other issues generally associated with church leadership, such as appropriate dress for women attending church meetings (1 Timothy 2:9–10); caring for the poor and needy (1 Timothy 5:1–16); how the elders should magnify their priesthood office (1 Timothy 5:17–25); a charge to preach the gospel (2 Timothy 4:2–5); and proper conduct after baptism (Titus 3:1–11).

Another consistent theme in the pastorals is the general apostasy that will precede the Savior's return. As previously mentioned, Paul had taught early in his career that perhaps he and others would still be alive when the Lord returned in power from heaven. Over the course of his service as a missionary, as his life was in jeopardy, he began to change his opinion about whether he would still be alive when the Savior came. By the time that he wrote the pastoral epistles, he had completely changed his opinion concerning whether he would live or whether any of the saints then living would be alive to meet Christ at His coming. A similar sentiment is preserved in the teachings of the Prophet Joseph Smith, who said, "Were I going to prophesy, I would say the end [of the world] would not come in 1844, 5, or 6, or in forty years. There are those of the rising generation who shall not taste death till Christ comes. I was once praying earnestly upon this subject, and a voice said unto me, 'My son, if thou livest until thou are eighty-five years of age, thou shalt see the face of the Son of Man.' I was left to draw my own conclusions concerning this; and I took the liberty to conclude that if I did live to that time, He would make His appearance. But I do not say whether He will make His appearance or I shall go where He is" (Dahl and Cannon, *Encyclopedia of Joseph Smith's Teachings*, 623).

Paul taught Timothy, "This know also, that in the last days perilous times shall come. . . . But thou hast fully known my doctrine, manner of life, purpose, faith, longsuffering, charity, patience, persecutions, afflictions, which came unto me at Antioch, at Iconium, at Lystra; what persecutions I endured: but out of them all the Lord delivered me. Yea, and *all that will live godly in Christ Jesus shall suffer persecution*" (2 Timothy 3:1,10–12; emphasis added). Paul now expected that all the saints would suffer as he had, and that the dark night of persecution would soon overtake the church.

Some of the details of that coming apostasy were described in his first letter to Timothy, where he said, "Now the Spirit speaketh expressly, that in the latter times some shall depart from the faith, giving heed to seducing spirits, and doctrines of devils" (1 Timothy 4:1). His statements to Timothy are reminiscent of Luke's report of what Paul taught the elders of Ephesus when they met him at Miletus: "For I know this, that after my departing shall grievous wolves enter in among you, not sparing the flock. Also of your own selves shall men arise, speaking perverse things, to draw away disciples after them" (Acts 20:29–30). The great weight bearing down on his soul during his final years resulted from his understanding of how the effects of apostasy would rupture the church and lead away those with whom he had worked for so many years. He was also concerned that his close friends, Timothy and Titus, would similarly be affected by the impending apostasy, or that persecution could drive them from their course. Paul expressed this same concern to the Romans, saying, "Who shall separate us from the love of Christ? shall tribulation, or distress, or persecution, or famine, or nakedness, or peril, or sword?" (Romans 8:35).

Paul knew that his own time was short and that he now faced his final imprisonment, but his work, he feared, would be undone after his departure. He had been a stalwart example to numerous congregations of saints throughout the entire eastern Mediterranean region, but as his final epistles reveal, each of the branches was facing severe persecution and intrigue. Given Paul's epistles alone, one could easily arrive at the conclusion that Paul's suspicions were confirmed and that the forces of darkness prevailed after his departure. Today it is difficult to ascertain how those struggling branches of the church fared after his death, but if his letters give any indication, they almost certainly stumbled and fell.

Some have wondered why no account was ever given of Paul's death. Modern societies are more fascinated with the details of death than were their ancient counterparts. In telling the life of a hero, it was not uncommon to simply pass over the details of his death. Paul was certainly a hero for Luke, to the extent that he shaped the way Luke told the entire history of the church after A.D. 35. The history of the church became the history of Paul. Paul died in Rome, having been found guilty of treason or some other trumped-up charge that had proven successful in suppressing other members of this new Messianic movement from Galilee.

Tradition reports that Paul suffered martyrdom under Nero, "So it came about that this man [Nero], the first to be heralded as a conspicuous fighter against God, was led on to murder the apostles. It is recorded that in his reign Paul was beheaded in Rome itself" (Eusebius, *Church History,* 2.25). In a later, more dubious account, it is reported, "In Rome, then, Nero was (raging) at the instigation of the evil one, many Christians being put to death without trial, so that the Romans took their stand at the palace and cried: 'It is enough Caesar! . . . Then he made an end (of the persecution). . . . Then Paul was brought before him in accordance with the decree, and he adhered to the decision that he should be beheaded . . . after communing in prayer in Hebrew with the fathers he stretched out his neck without speaking further . . . [then] the executioner struck off his head" (*Acts of Paul,* 11).

Perhaps such reports would satisfy modern curiosities, but at the same time they detract from Luke's greater intent of reporting the life of his hero. Paul gave his own report of his death when he told Timothy, "For I am now ready to be offered, and the time of my departure is at hand. I have fought a good fight, I have finished my course, I have kept the faith: Henceforth there is laid up for me a crown of righteousness, which the Lord, the righteous judge, shall give me at that day: and not to me only, but unto all them also that love his appearing. . . . And the Lord shall deliver me from every evil work, and will preserve me unto his heavenly kingdom: to whom be glory for ever and ever. Amen" (2 Timothy 4:6–8, 18). Paul gave his own account of his death, one without the sting and pain of departure. Paul knew that he would be saved in the kingdom of God as so many other prophets who had gone before him. For Luke to narrate the details of his death would only serve to remind everyone of the short-lived victory achieved by his opponents in taking his life.

Having lived his life in Christ, the pains of death were nothing more than a peripheral concern. In fact, his death opened the door to a glorious reunion that Paul had anxiously sought for more than thirty years. He had seen the Lord at the beginning of his mission, and he now had the privilege of seeing him again. Paul wanted us to focus on the victory rather than the momentary setback of death. As Paul stated many years earlier: "We have this treasure in earthen vessels, that the excellency of the power may be of God, and not of us. We are troubled on every side, yet not distressed" (2 Corinthians 4:7–8). How can death claim victory if it opens the way to eternal, glorious existence in the presence of our Lord and Savior? Paul was now with God, and his closing words to Timothy leave the impression that Paul lived on eternally, a fitting end to the life of a hero.

WORKS CITED

ANCIENT SOURCES

Note: All references in the text to ancient sources can be found in the respective English translations.

Acts of Paul

Wilhelm Schneemelcher, ed. *New Testament Apocrypha.* 2 vols. Louisville: Westminster/John Knox Press, 1992.

Apostolic Fathers

Bart D. Ehrman, ed. and trans. *The Apostolic Fathers.* 2 vols. Cambridge, Mass., and London: Harvard University, 2003.

Babylonian Talmud

Jacob Neusner, trans. *The Talmud of Babylonia: An American Translation.* Brown Judaic Studies 268–69. Atlanta: Scholars Press, 1992.

Birkhat ha-minim

David Instone-Brewer. "The Eighteen Benedictions and the *Minim* Before 70 CE." *Journal of Theological Studies* 54 (2003): 31.

Celsus

W. G. Spencer, trans. *Celsus.* 3 vols. Cambridge Mass., and London: Harvard University, 1971.

Cicero

L. H. G. Greenwood, trans. *Cicero.* 28 vols. Cambridge Mass., and London: Harvard University, 1976.

Epictetus

W. A. Oldfather, trans. *The Discourses as Reported by Arrian; The manual; And fragments.* 2 vols. Cambridge, Mass., and London: Harvard University, 1925.

Epiphanius

Frank Williams, trans. *Panarion.* Leiden: Brill, 1994.

Eusebius

G. A. Williamson, trans. *Eusebius.* rev. ed. Andrew Louth, London: Penguin Books, 1989.

Jerome

Philip Schaff and Henry Wace, eds. *A Select Library of Nicene and Post-Nicene Fathers of the Christian Church.* 10 vols. trans. E. C. Richardson. Grand Rapids, Mich.: Eerdmans, 1979.

Josephus

William Whiston, trans. *The Works of Josephus.* Peabody, Mass.: Hendrickson, 1987.

Juvenal

Susanna Morton Braund, trans. *Juvenal and Persius.* Cambridge, Mass., and London: Harvard University, 2004.

Lucian

A. M. Harmon, trans., *Lucian.* 8 vols. Cambridge, Mass., and London: Harvard University, 1972.

Philo

C. D. Yonge, trans. *The Works of Philo.* Peabody, Mass.: Hendrickson, 1993.

Philostratus

Jeffrey Henderson, trans. *Philostratus.* 2 vols. Cambridge, Mass., and London: Harvard University, 2005.

Pliny

W. H. S. Jones, trans. *Pliny.* 10 vols. Cambridge, Mass., and London: Harvard University, 1963.

Plutarch

Bernadotte Perrin, trans. *Plutarch.* 11 vols. Cambridge, Mass., and London: Harvard University, 1961.

Seneca

Richard M. Gummere, trans. *Ad Lucilium epistulae morales.* 3 vols. Cambridge, Mass., and London: Harvard University, 1917.

Strabo

Horace Leonard Jones, trans. *Strabo.* 8 vols. Cambridge, Mass., and London: Harvard University, 2000.

Suetonius

J. C. Rolfe, trans. *Suetonius.* 2 vols. Cambridge, Mass., and London: Harvard University, 1970.

Tacitus

John Jackson, trans. *Tacitus.* 5 vols. Cambridge, Mass., and London: Harvard University, 1998.

MODERN SOURCES

Gordon B. Hinckley. *Teachings of Gordon B. Hinckley.* Salt Lake City: Deseret Book, 1997.

Jeffrey R. Holland. *Trusting Jesus.* Salt Lake City: Deseret Book, 2003.

David O. McKay. *Steppingstones to an Abundant Life.* Salt Lake City: Deseret Book, 1971.

LeGrand Richards. In Conference Report, April 1956, 94–98.

Joseph Fielding Smith. *Answers to Gospel Questions.* 4 vols. Salt Lake City: Deseret Book, 1963.

Joseph Smith. *Encyclopedia of Joseph Smith's Teachings.* Edited by Larry E. Dahl and Donald Q. Cannon. Salt Lake City: Deseret Book, 1997.

———. *Teachings of the Prophet Joseph Smith.* Selected by Joseph Fielding Smith. Salt Lake City: Deseret Book, 1976.

Orson F. Whitney. In Conference Report, October 1912, 68–73.

SOURCES FOR CHAPTER HEADING QUOTES

Chapter 1: Jeffrey R. Holland, *Trusting Jesus,* 46.

Chapter 2: Joseph Fielding Smith, *Answers to Gospel Questions,* 4:10.

Chapter 3: Joseph Smith, *Teachings of the Prophet Joseph Smith,* 63.

Chapter 4: Joseph Smith, *Teachings of the Prophet Joseph Smith,* 180.

Chapter 5: Orson F. Whitney, in Conference Report, October 1912, 70–71.

Chapter 6: LeGrand Richards, in Conference Report, April 1956, 95–96.

Chapter 7: Gordon B. Hinckley, *Teachings of Gordon B. Hinckley,* 197–98.

Chapter 8: David O. McKay, *Steppingstones to an Abundant Life,* 41.

INDEX